Marinas

The Complete Guide for Marina
Selection, Storm Awareness and Living
Comfortably Aboard Your Yacht

By
Scott E. McDowell

USCG Licensed Captain and Ph.D. Oceanographer

MARINAS: The Complete Guide for Marina Selection, Storm Awareness and Living Comfortably Aboard Your Yacht

Published by: Atlantic Publishing Group, Inc.
1405 SW 6th Avenue • Ocala, Florida 34471 • Phone 800-814-1132 • Fax 352-622-1875
Web site: www.atlantic-pub.com • E-mail: sales@atlantic-pub.com
SAN Number: 268-1250

Library of Congress Cataloging-in-Publication Data

McDowell, Scott E.
  Marinas : the complete guide for marina selection, storm awareness and living comfortably aboard your yacht / by Scott E. McDowell.
    pages cm
  ISBN 978-1-62023-087-9 (alk. paper) -- ISBN 1-62023-087-9 (alk. paper) 1. Marinas--United States. 2. Boat living--United States. I. Title. II. Title: Complete guide for marina selection, storm awareness and living comfortably aboard your yacht.
  VK369.5.M37 2015
  643'.2--dc23
                          2015011940

EDITOR: Melissa Shortman • mfigueroa@atlantic-pub.com
COVER & INTERIOR DESIGN: Meg Buchner • megadesn@mchsi.com

Cover Photo Courtesy of Longboat Key Club Moorings. 27.36744 N.82.61936 W.
Photos on pages 22, 135, 246 and 253 Courtesy of Lloyd Wilkonson

Printed on Recycled Paper

Printed in the United States

Reduce. Reuse.
RECYCLE.

A decade ago, Atlantic Publishing signed the Green Press Initiative. These guidelines promote environmentally friendly practices, such as using recycled stock and vegetable-based inks, avoiding waste, choosing energy-efficient resources, and promoting a no-pulping policy. We now use 100-percent recycled stock on all our books. The results: in one year, switching to post-consumer recycled stock saved 24 mature trees, 5,000 gallons of water, the equivalent of the total energy used for one home in a year, and the equivalent of the greenhouse gases from one car driven for a year.

Over the years, we have adopted a number of dogs from rescues and shelters. First there was Bear and after he passed, Ginger and Scout. Now, we have Kira, another rescue. They have brought immense joy and love not just into our lives, but into the lives of all who met them.

We want you to know a portion of the profits of this book will be donated in Bear, Ginger and Scout's memory to local animal shelters, parks, conservation organizations, and other individuals and nonprofit organizations in need of assistance.

*— **Douglas & Sherri Brown**,*
President & Vice-President of Atlantic Publishing

· DISCLAIMER ·

This guidebook describes many features and procedures common to marinas along all U.S. coasts as well as in the Great Lakes. Specifications of individual marinas are purposely not given, as they can be obtained directly from marinas and their websites. Marina information also can be obtained from independent Marina websites whose purpose is to aid boaters in identifying marinas throughout the U.S.

Although every effort has been made to provide accurate information, the author and publisher do not take responsibility for errors, incorrect information or omissions. Similarly, any websites given herein may not be active at the time of reader's query and this is not the author's responsibility.

The author and publisher have neither liability nor responsibility to any person or entity with respect to any loss or damage caused, or alleged to be caused, directly or indirectly by the information contained in this book.

The purpose of this guidebook is to help boaters evaluate various marinas for suitability of their vessel and personal lifestyle. Additionally, this book educates the reader on oceanographic processes and storms that can impact the marina and the owner's vessel. Hopefully new boaters as well as experienced captains can gain from the information provided herein.

• DEDICATION •

To my Great-Great-Grandfather, Samuel McDowell who emigrated from Scotland to Dennis, Massachusetts where most of my paternal family live today. Born in 1803, he spent much of his life on the sea, raising a hardy family on the shores of Cape Cod Bay. The 1860 Census in the Town of Dennis identifies Samuel succinctly as "Mariner" and it's his salty blood that I carry in my veins today.

His Grandson Walter, my Grandfather, purchased a special plot of high ground in north Dennis that spanned from Scargo Lake to Cape Cod Bay, upon which many generations of strong-minded McDowells were spawned. That land was within a quarter mile of Samuel's initial plot. Walter walked the Bay shore each day, remembering Samuel on the same clam flats 100 years before.

I died of total cardiac arrest in February 2007 while ice-skating on the same Scargo Lake with my daughter and cousin. She and Dennis firemen 'worked me hard' for nearly 30 minutes until the ambulance arrived and used a defibrillator to finally get a pulse. Thank you all for not giving up on me as I lay lifeless on the ice that cold day.

During my recovery, my uncle Peter graciously took me into his home (previously Walter's) situated on a sand dune overlooking the shore where Samuel and Walter walked. I walked the same flats during my convalescence, thinking of Samuel being the first. His footprints were long since washed away, as will mine.

My entire family fueled my recovery and we remain very close today. I am now living in "My Heaven" with my loving wife Susan aboard my yacht. Samuel's love of the sea continues, in me and within my children too. Six generations of McDowells from the shores of Cape Cod Bay.

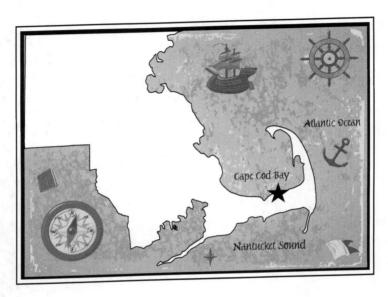

• ACKNOWLEDGMENTS •

I wish to acknowledge a variety of people, places and things that led me to who I am and why the ocean has always been so important to me. It's why I greatly enjoyed writing this book. Starting with a few *things*:

- The smell of tar on my fingers from grasping the handline and landing my first flounder while fishing as a young boy with my Grandfather in Cape Cod Bay.

- The blue smoke and familiar oily smell from the two-cycle outboard engines aboard wooden skiffs we'd take for dangerous rides in Sesuit Harbor as boys.

- The salty taste of a raw sea clam freshly dug from the sand flats of Cape Cod Bay on a January morning, while looking at my Grandfather in his tall waders.

- The screaming sound as the giant Bluefin tuna stole a quarter-mile of line off the smoking Penn fishing reel. We landed him in four hours, all 665 pounds, and won the Cape Cod Tuna Tournament in 1969, our first year in the competition.

Special *places* that each contributed to my personal development:

- The 212-foot Research Vessel Chain that was home during my first job at the Woods Hole Oceanographic Institution – a 7-month research cruise to the South Atlantic and Antarctic Oceans – and my first experience in 30-foot seas.

- The delivery rooms where my two wonderful children were born, as I witnessed in awe and heard their first gasps.

- Discovering the very first "Meddy", a deep mid-ocean eddy of Mediterranean Sea origin swirling one mile below the surface, as I was surveying 100 miles offshore The Bahamas for my Ph.D. research.

- Scargo Lake in Dennis, near my childhood home and where I died 'the first time'.

Most importantly, I wish to thank the ***people*** who provided encouragement and purpose for my writing.

First, I thank Doug Brown and his excellent team at Atlantic Publishing, Inc. He dared to extend a publishing contract to me, an unpublished author. His love for boating fortunately softened his 'acceptance guidelines' for new authors.

To Jack Watson, a good friend who encouraged me to write, write and then write more. His introduction to Doug and Atlantic Publishing, Inc. made it all happen.

To Neil Ross who graciously reviewed the draft manuscript and wrote the Foreword for this book. I am honored to receive his review which is solidly based on his 30 years working in the Global Marina Industry, walking the docks of nearly 1,000 marinas in 26 nations and most States in the U.S. He's certainly the Professor of Marinas.

To my interesting and daring friends who cruise the seven seas aboard research ships studying the ocean and its seafloor. Our long days of blue-water oceanography at high and low latitudes sit fondly in my memories. The salt water in your veins certainly deserves the occasional transfusion with Goslings rum.

To my mother at the graduation ceremony for my Ph.D. in Oceanography, who smiled and reminded me that the Nun for my fifth-grade class at parochial school told her that "little Scotty is slow" which meant 'stupid' in those days.

My son, Zachery, and daughter, Danielle, who grew to appreciate the challenges faced by untrained parents, especially the father whose patience was often eroded by his workday, leaving little energy for night-time storytelling. I'm still 'Dad' to them but as adults we now share wonderful conversation about personal development and what's really important in life. They know writing puts me in a good place.

Susan, my loving partner and wife, deserves the most thanks for her continued encouragement for my writing. When my literary prowess and confidence would wane, she'd sternly say "You are a writer" to reset my focus. Productivity is my driver but her 'P' word is perfection as demonstrated each time she would edit my scratchy sentences, fortunately for my readers. Thank you Susan.

· TABLE OF CONTENTS ·

CHAPTER 4: Marina Essentials   73

CHAPTER 5: Tides　　　　91

CHAPTER 6: Marina Facilities – Important Issues　　97

CHAPTER 7: Other Marina Considerations 113

CHAPTER 8: Vessel Considerations and Services   135

CHAPTER 10: Storm Considerations   179

CHAPTER 13: Marina Tenant Agreements   235

CHAPTER 14: Buying and Selling a Yacht   247

References   253

Glossary   257

Author Biography   281

Index   283

• FOREWORD •

This book, *Marinas: The Complete Guide for Marina Selection, Storm Awareness and Living Comfortably Aboard Your Yacht* is for you, the boat owner, and I am happy to write this foreword. This is the second foreword I've written for a marina book. That other is the technical engineering and design book "Marinas and Small Craft Harbors" published for marina industry professionals, owners, managers, engineers, and government regulators. Interestingly both books are similar on marina physical characteristics, sites, tides, weather, and environment.

First time and skilled boaters will find many useful tips and information in this easy to read reference book by Scott McDowell. Each chapter is based on his boating experiences while visiting and living aboard at many marinas around the United States. His writing style is conversational, practical, and at times humorous.

The author teaches many things about marinas, social to legal, including a layman's guide to the all-important natural and physical forces that can affect any boat's safety, comfort, and use. As he states, each marina is unique in its management style, site, services, and customer mix.

The book clearly focuses on you; the boat user who Scott calls the tenant. As a tenant you are subject to the same regulations imposed on the marina by national, state, and local government laws and regulations. Insurance companies also add contractual restrictions on how the business can operate safely and avoid lawsuits. Each marina adds its own regulations for site-specific safe, clean, controlled boat operation and conduct of tenants and guests.

Most marinas, however, will likely call you a *customer*, *boat owner*, *captain*, or *member*. In recent decades the American marina industry changed the way it looks at itself. Instead of being places where boats are stored and used, many forward thinking marina managers see themselves more focused on serving customers than on the vessels and will often call you their guest.

I agree with Scott about correlation between cost of the marina and service/experience quality. He explains how you can find very inexpensive, even cheap, marinas in most markets, but on close examination those facilities likely have problems that can curtail your boat use, limit the size/height/depth of the vessel, or offer really poor quality of experience. His observation that often the highest cost marinas in a market can also be the best place for your boat and use. The exception, he points out, is that decent government owned marinas are relatively inexpensive, have the slowest turn over, and longest waiting lists.

What was fun for me while reading this interesting book was being able to visualize all the good and bad examples described to actual marinas I've visited.

I highly recommend *Marinas: The Complete Guide for Marina Selection, Storm Awareness and Living Comfortably Aboard Your Yacht* for any serious cruising boater or one seeking a new long-term place to berth your boat.

Neil W. Ross
Kingston, Rhode Island

Neil Ross has professionally visited nearly 1,000 marinas in 16 nations and 42 states/territories giving him a wide view of world marinas. He is widely recognized as the founding leader of the International Marina Institute, Marine Environmental Education Foundation, National Clean Marina & Clean Boating Programs, Certified Marina Manager accreditation, co-author of US EPA's National Marina & Boating Environmental Guidelines, and international trainer to thousands of marina industry leaders, trade associations, federal and state coastal regulators, author of hundreds of marina related documents, and currently writing monthly marina history articles for the national trade magazine Marina Dock Age.

• CHAPTER 1 •
Introduction and Boater Statistics

Maritime captains and 'boaters' in general are prolific storytellers, always eager to swamp a willing ear. Undoubtedly, those with gray beards and absent fingers tell the most perilous tales. The only commonality among these 'salty yarns' is their ending: "If only I had known when ... how ...". Even with these warnings and recommendations you'll likely encounter unpredictable, dangerous situations of your own as you venture seaward.

Today dozens of guidebooks and websites address boating topics such as purchasing a vessel, seamanship, safety at sea, vessel maintenance and selecting cruising destinations. Perilous stories abound on these topics too.

Fortunately, valuable information is also provided to reduce risk for the nautical readership.

This guidebook addresses a significant information gap in maritime literature, specifically, 'How To' select the optimum marina for dockage of your vessel. Whether you own a small sloop, a high-powered sportfishing boat, a live-aboard trawler or a modern mega-yacht, this book identifies key marina issues to consider before signing your next marina tenant agreement. Real marina situations are discussed and accompanied by anecdotes of 'what not to do' in certain circumstances. Equally significant is a large chapter that educates boaters on the storm processes than can affect marinas and ruin your vessel. Specifics on facilities and guidelines of individual marinas are purposely not given.

With this quick read, new boaters can learn the tricks and odd jargon of marina life. For partners who live aboard, this book should be essential reading by all so captain and mate have a common understanding of boating terminology. Furthermore, even with an experienced captain aboard, don't assume he/she has considered all factors associated with a particular marina or approaching storm. Know what's necessary and keep your captain on his/her toes.

The author's goal is to educate by example with a bit of added humor and sea salt. Remember that it's you, the vessel owner, who encounters the inconveniences and eats the financial consequences.

Boater Profiles and Vessel Statistics

One of the joys of boating and marina life is the variety of people you meet. No two boaters are alike and their stories and backgrounds differ widely. All you have in common is a love for the sea (or lake or river) upon which you seek recreation, relaxation or commerce. This sounds romantic but that's not the whole picture. Actually, you need to realize that some seafarers and vessel operators don't love their vessel or the sea; they just do it for a living, some even resentfully. That's okay and we all must acknowledge it's their prerogative and sometimes their necessity. Most importantly, don't try to change anyone's attitude while they're boating. They are entitled to be as friendly or grizzly as they wish, so long as they're not extremely offensive and/or dangerous to others. Everyone must abide by marina rules and U.S. Coast Guard Rules of the Road (2014) when on the water. That's the extent of what's permissible, acceptable and necessary. Other than that, keep your attitude to yourself at sea, on the marine radio and at the dock.

The diversity of persons and personalities who could become your marina neighbor is equally extraordinary. Books could be written about all the quirky individuals but that's certainly beyond the scope of this guidebook.

BOATER PROFILES FROM 2015 MARINAS.COM SURVEY

The marina-search website Marinas.com allows visitors to search for marina facilities throughout the U.S. Additionally, that organization has compiled interesting boater statistics from a survey completed by many of its members (2015). Relevant results are given below:

- More than 50 percent of the respondents have been boating for more than 20 years whereas 20 percent have been boating five or fewer years.

- 42 percent of the respondents have owned three or more boats, while 48 percent have owned one or two boats; 10 percent have not owned boats but they participated on the Marinas.com website, likely considering vessel purchase.

- 38 percent of the respondents have owned motor yachts or trawlers; 33 percent owned sportfishing or center-console boats; 29 percent owned sail boats; 13 percent have not owned boats; only 2 percent have owned catamarans (power or sail).

- Cruising and relaxation were the highest uses (78 percent and 72 percent, respectively); fishing second (42 percent) while other water-sports were less frequent for respondents. It's likely that owners of only Personal Water Craft do not have need to visit marina websites.

- Regarding size of vessel owned, only 5 percent of respondents ever owned vessels longer than 50 feet; 66 percent of respondents had largest vessels between 21 and 40 feet.

- Two-thirds of the boaters operated in salt-water environments.

- One-quarter of the respondents expect to purchase another boat more than six months in the future.

- Respondents are 2.5 times more likely to purchase a used boat than a new one.

- Respondents are more likely to purchase motor yachts and trawlers (a combined 32 percent) than sailboats (19 percent) or sportfishing boats (12 percent).

- Assuming respondents are honest, 52 percent claim their annual income exceeds $100,000. Only 19 percent claim they make less than $50,000 per year.

Interesting demographics but the statistical validity of these results has not been proven nor are the number of survey respondents indicated.

Statistics from Vessel Registrations

The U.S. Coast Guard compiles annual statistics from *recreational* vessels registered in all 50 States (USCG, Commandant Publication P16754.27; 2014). The data presented below represent statistics only for mechanically powered vessels and watercraft registered in 2013; unpowered vessels are not included but total 885,444 vessels.

Length of vessel (ft)	Number of registered vessels
< 16	4,405,152
16 - 25	6,158,252
26 - 40	481,353
41 – 65	69,280
> 65	14,015
TOTAL	**11,128,052**

Although 11 million registered recreational powered vessels is certainly a very large number, it appears that the actual number for vessels over 25 feet in length is greatly under-reported. As discussed in more detail below, most marinas cater to large vessels and there are likely over 1 million vessels over 25 feet berthed in marinas nationally. Furthermore, the Coast Guard data do not include large vessels that are federally documented (versus State registration). In Florida, it has been estimated that federally documented vessels are as prevalent as vessels with State registrations, which further supports the belief that the Coast Guard data are underestimated by at least a factor of two for large vessels.

The Coast Guard data from 2013 also indicate the geographic distribution of registered recreational vessels. States with the most registered vessels are identified below, given as percentages of the national total (12,013,496) for mechanically powered and non-powered vessels.

Geographic Distribution of Registered Recreational Vessels (Coast Guard Data 2013)		
STATE	%	# VESSELS
Florida	7.2%	870,749
California	6.8%	820,490
Minnesota	6.7%	808,744
Michigan	6.6%	795,875
Wisconsin	5.1%	613,516
Texas	4.8%	575,402

The large number of vessels in the Great Lakes region (although data for only Minnesota, Michigan and Wisconsin are shown above) is driven by the high percentage of small vessels in these States where boating is confined to lakes and rivers.

Another source of annual statistics for recreational vessels is the National Marine Manufacturers Association (NMMA). Their results for 2010, exclusive of federally documented vessels (as for the Coast Guard results) are below for the States having the highest number of registered recreational vessels.

Geographic Distribution of Registered Recreational Vessels NMMA Data 2010		
STATE	%	# VESSELS
Florida	7.3%	914,535
Minnesota	6.5%	813,976
Michigan	6.5%	812,066
California	6.5%	810,008
Wisconsin	4.9%	615,335
Texas	4.8%	596,830

Their survey totaled 12.5 million vessels for 2010, which is comparable to the Coast Guard results for 2013, and the data for individual States are similar also.

STATISTICS OF U.S. MARINAS

Numerous free websites allow users to search for marinas in specific cities, States or regions in the U.S. These sites are valuable tools for determining marina locations, general capabilities and points of contact – perfect for developing a 'short list' of marinas you should visit during the first round of your search. You'll often be surprised how many marinas exist, even in a harbor that you thought you knew well. These marina-search websites also represent a database from which interesting statistics can be mined with ease. For example, provided below are estimates of marinas in major U.S. regions, derived from marina information presented for individual States by Marinas.com (2015):

Marinas In The United States		
East Coast (including east coast of FL)	3,950+	63%
Gulf of Mexico (including west coast of FL)	550+	9%
Great Lakes and major inland States (excluding NY)	900+	14%
West Coast (including HI; excluding AK)	850+	14%
Total number of marinas in the U.S.	6,250+	

- East Coast has nearly five times more marinas than the West Coast, likely for two reasons: higher coastal population and the large number of bays, coves and harbors of refuge compared to the rugged coastline of the Pacific shore.

- Great Lakes marinas are comparable with the number of West Coast marinas

- Gulf of Mexico has the smallest number of marinas for regions delineated

States with largest numbers of marinas	
Florida	980
New York	900
California	480
New Jersey	450
Maryland	430
Michigan	420
Massachusetts	400

- Florida and New York, combined, host 30 percent of all U.S. marinas

For boating novices, these statistics support the belief that marinas abound and there will be many to choose from when they purchase their dream vessel. A buyer's market they might imagine.

Mr. Neil Ross, who wrote the foreword for this book, had conducted a national inventory of U.S. marinas in collaboration with State Sea Grant offices in the late 1980s. His survey revealed more than 8,000 marine facilities but this higher number (in comparison with the recent Marinas.com survey) could have partly been due to boatyards being included in the Ross inventory assessment, whereas the Marinas.com survey did not include boatyards that do not provide berths for recreational vessels.

It's Not a Sure Thing, Finding a Good Slip

A well-groomed man in his 50s walks into a seaside bar and orders a drink: "Dark 'N Stormy and make it a double with the Goslings."

Seeing that the patron is emotionally beaten, the bartender asks "What's got you so down fella?"

"This week was the best in my life ... and the worst." The man shakes his head from side to side then takes a long swig of his drink.

"How's that? You look like a successful man."

"On Tuesday I closed the deal on my 54-ft Fleming motor yacht. She's fantastic. But today when I visited my vessel, the Dock Master informed me I have to move her out of the slip by tomorrow ... and the marina has no other slips my size."

This scenario is not unrealistic, especially for those buying their first yacht or upgrading from a relatively small, trailered boat without having thought about dockage. In some cases the newly purchased, pre-owned vessel is berthed at a distant marina or it may be a new purchase at a boat show. Other times, the vessel may be docked in the ideal location for the new owner but the sale does not include a continuation of the existing marina tenant agreement.

Rarely does anyone involved in the sale of a vessel, yacht broker, surveyor or past owner, ask where you intend to dock your new prize – sometimes an intentional oversight. In doing so they might just reveal that it's often difficult (or impossible) to find a berth in the marina of your choice, especially if the vessel is large (i.e., greater than 50 feet) or very wide such as with catamarans.

Begin Your Marina Search Before You Purchase Your Vessel

As soon as you know the approximate length of the vessel you may purchase, that's the time to begin your search for a marina. Here are my recommendations:

- Decide which harbors would be acceptable for your vessel and don't limit yourself to a single harbor if there are other options within a reasonable driving distance. Start with a broad search.

- Go online to select one of the Marina Search websites such as **Marinas.com** or **ActiveCaptain.com** then conduct searches for marinas in your preferred geography to identify those that may be viable options.

- Visit each marina's website and evaluate their specific capabilities and amenities. **Read this guidebook first so you know how to thoroughly evaluate a marina.**

- Make a short list of those marinas that appear to meet your general needs.

- **Don't call them to ask about availability of slips.**

- Drive to each, walk around the facility and speak with marina personnel regarding issues important to you.

- Inspect the marina's bathroom facilities for boaters, as they are an excellent indicator of marina maintenance and cleanliness. As trivial as this may sound, it is one of the key criteria that many boaters use in their final selection of a marina.

- **Be cooperative and friendly. Keep in mind that you should be selling yourself to them, not the other way around. Remember, they make the final decision whether you and your vessel will enter their marina.**

If You Already Own a Vessel

Seasoned boaters who already own a vessel sometimes want a change in geography, either while cruising or for warmer climes during retirement years. The optimum marina is essential for you to fully enjoy the boating experience. Although you may have learned a great deal about what constitutes your key marina needs, use this guidebook to consider amenities you may not have encountered at your present facility. Be a wise shopper and follow the simple steps above to conduct your next marina search.

CHAPTER 2

Interaction with Marina Management

Cooperation

No two marinas are alike, especially regarding management personnel and procedures. A common management hierarchy includes a dock-master who manages day-to-day operations of the dock facilities including any support staff such as dock boys', fuel-dock personnel, etc. Dockmasters are the key individuals to contact if you have an operational question (i.e., electric, water, etc.) or need a task performed by marina support personnel. Most importantly, they decide when the marina rules can be bent; for example, may you lease Slip A-4 even though your transom will extend six feet beyond the end of the pier? Always get on the 'good side' of the dock-master because they govern the physical operations at the marina. There are myriad other ways they can make your boating life easier but more on that later.

> ## • AUTHOR OBSERVATION •
>
> *In this and other chapters that address the contract between a boat owner and a marina, the term tenant has been used synonymously with boat owner. This formality does not exist in verbal communication at marinas; in fact it's just the opposite situation as marinas have, in recent years, recognized the importance of 'customer focus'. Consequently, marina personnel typically address boaters as owner, member or captain with friendly respect for their customers, which they need to keep.*

Marina management personnel run the business aspects of the marina, primarily from a financial and contractual standpoint. They facilitate your marina tenant agreement, monitor your electrical usage (if necessary), assure continuous electric, water, cable service, trash removal, sewage pump-out, landscaping, etc. They also approve and oversee subcontractors rendering on-site services.

Quite often there will be an esteemed marina manager with a cadre of administrative support personnel. For small and/or efficiently run marinas, the full complement of office staff may total two to four personnel and the manager is often accessible at the front desk for informal discussion and negotiations. Sometimes the manager also doubles as the dockmaster, making final decisions on slip assignment and scheduling. On your first arrival at the marina be sure to establish a respectful, cooperative business relationship with the manager and assure him/her you'll not be a 'high maintenance' tenant. Prove that you are knowledgeable about boating and marina life so you're viewed as a potential asset to the facility.

If you are relatively new to boating and marina life, be honest and explain this to the manager and dockmaster. Ask them whether the marina community has boaters who would enjoy teaching you about various essentials of boating. Coast Guard Power Squadron members may also be an excellent source of training for new boaters.

Most marinas have a waiting list for boats needing a slip. Some marina managers will even show you a long list of names to support their claim that "It'll be a while before we could find a slip for you in our marina. Try contacting me in six months and we'll put you near the top of the wait list." This fair and objective, first-come-first-served (FCFS) process is used for slip assignments in many marinas, especially those that are city-run where all decisions are purposely kept 'black and white'; no favoritism allowed. But don't let this fool you into thinking that slip assignment is a 'fair' process everywhere.

Managers at some marinas have an unwritten, subjective process that violates the FCFS waiting list concept. Case in point: many angry boat owners rightly claim they've been on the list at their favorite marina for years with no success and their anger grows each time they hear another boater has been assigned a slip soon after their initial inquiry. How unfair on the part of the marina manager.

Hold your judgment. Let's first look at this situation from the manager's standpoint. He/she has encountered hundreds, maybe thousands of boaters during their marina management career and certainly developed skills to quickly assess the knowledge, boating capabilities and cooperation of these boaters from an initial conversation or two. In many cases, prospective tenants do an excellent job demonstrating their lack of boating knowledge within the first few minutes of discussion with marina personnel.

Worse yet, the prospective tenant's lack of patience glows brighter each time he/she calls the manager to inquire whether their slip is now available. The manager doesn't have to be a Ph.D. Psychologist to categorize this individual as 'high maintenance' and likely a liability to his staff and the marina community. Accordingly, the manager mentally keeps this applicant near the bottom of his 'real list', never to be next in line for a slip.

"Golly, this is downright unfair." Actually not – it's an example of a 'seasoned' marina manager using their screening ability to keep potentially disruptive boaters out of their marina community. They're doing a favor for the boating community, as well as preventing marina employees from having to receive grief from a never-content tenant.

For boaters who are disgruntled because they're on the receiving end of this 'blackball' process, they should conserve their energy and obtain counseling on how to better interact with private business representatives. (In the old days they'd call this attending Charm School.) When a prospective tenant is patient, cooperative and respectful of marina management and their policies, they'll usually obtain a slip quicker than other less-cooperative applicants. I know from personal experience at multiple marinas on both U.S. coasts.

After you've become a tenant, the next step is to develop a respectful working relationship with marina support staff because they are the eyes and ears of the manager. They can be very helpful with many small marina issues but on the other side of the coin, if they see or hear a tenant is breaking the rules or being difficult, word gets to the manager immediately and you may soon be questioned. As petty as it sounds, some marina tenants try to get cozy with marina management by squealing on tenants who are violating marina policies, even if the matter is relatively insignificant. You can normally spot these spies who are always looking around but not saying much.

Live-Aboard and Occupancy Considerations

Many marinas don't allow tenants to live aboard, period. This may be their own decision or one imposed by local, state or federal regulations based upon pollution guidelines. Even though marinas prohibit discharge of treated or untreated sewage (nautically referred to as 'black water') into their waters, live-aboard vessels discharge considerable volumes of 'gray water' from sinks, dishwashers, shower sump pumps and pollutant-free bilges. Additionally they contribute lots of freshwater to the harbor during frequent hull-washing rituals. All of this liquid discharge certainly changes the chemistry of the natural receiving water in the harbor, with the effect of reducing water clarity and sometimes inducing nuisance algae blooms on account of excess nutrients being discharged. If the harbor is insufficiently flushed by tidal and/or river flows, water quality can degrade significantly with numerous live-aboard vessels fueling the problem.

Marinas situated in harbors with limited flushing are typically limited to a certain percentage of slips for live-aboard tenants, some as low as 20 percent. Consequently, if you are planning to live aboard initially or at some time in the future, it's essential that you determine the marina's guidelines on live-aboard slip quotas. Convey your short- and long-term plans to marina management early on, so they can give you their best guess about live-aboard slip availability.

Marinas offering live-aboard slips typically prevent these vessels from being berthed side-by-side, primarily for noise and privacy considerations, but don't count on this. Always walk the docks and view the location of your potential slip to see if there are any undesirable live-aboard vessels close to your future home. It's best to discuss this with marina management before you sign a tenant agreement. Also, ask them if you could move to a different slip at some time in the future if your neighbor becomes a problem. It's best to learn early on whether management is flexible and understanding of tenants' needs.

Even if you don't intend to live aboard full-time, most boaters like to spend an occasional night or two aboard their vessel. Fortunately, marinas generally allow this. The limit of overnight occupancy is defined by each marina tenant agreement so read the fine-print carefully as violations can sometimes lead to eviction — not a good situation if there isn't another marina nearby with slip availability for your vessel size.

Marinas normally allow tenants to sleep aboard for two nights each week but no more than five nights per month. They can, however, differ on temporary occupancy regulations as do the 'watchdogs' who report violators. At one marina there were many long-standing vessel tenants who would inform the marina manager if a neighbor had been aboard more than two consecutive nights. As mentioned above, these truly were spies hoping to gain the favor of marina management for their unsolicited surveillance services. It certainly contributed to a poor attitude in the neighborhood. From my perspective, the bigger problem was that the manager had established a type of military rule as if all tenants were under watchdog surveillance 24/7. Security from outside risks is necessary but a trustworthy neighborhood is paramount.

Wise marina management personnel encourage an active community of happy tenants and some facilities sponsor regular events such as periodic cookouts and holiday parties. These gatherings can be both enjoyable and informative as fellow boaters share local information and sources for goods and nautical services. Most certainly, there will be boaters eager to share their sea stories and live-board experiences.

Marina life can be grand if you like your neighbors but if your marina has numerous 'derelict' boats that are in major disrepair, the situation can be less than wonderful. Sadly, some boat owners live aboard because they cannot afford shore-side accommodations, nor can they pay for routine maintenance to keep their vessel operable and acceptable to the eye. If you see such vessels as you are making your initial walk around a new marina, ask marina management about their policy on vessel 'operability'. At a minimum, good marinas require each tenant vessel to start their engine(s) and move the vessel out of the slip at least once annually to demonstrate operability. Tell the manager that you've noticed that M/V Sight for Sore Eyes is a real 'rust bucket' and see if they intend to force vessel upgrades or eventual eviction. If they have no concern, that will tell you 'Captain Bligh' will never be forced to clean up his act; good luck to his neighbors.

Other live-aboard tenants prefer to live a quiet life, free of nautical 'small talk' each time they walk down the dock. If that's you, inquire whether you could lease a slip amongst the non-live-aboard boats, especially if they are much larger than your vessel. Interestingly, the largest long-term-berthed yachts in a marina are often not live-aboard vessels and are seldom used. Those over 70 feet in length, including the mega-yachts, are typically toys of the wealthy and many are used infrequently. If you don't need daily conversation from local live-aboards, berthing amongst large non-live-aboard vessels is the quietest situation you can find. Similarly, leasing a slip amongst large For Sale yachts can offer a quiet lifestyle too. These highly expensive vessels are seldom visited by prospective buyers and only during daylight hours with the eager broker in the lead.

In summary, being a good marina tenant is all about cooperation and your attitude is essential. Conversely, if you're a demanding tenant, you'll find yourself being eased out quicker than you can imagine because slip assignment can be a very subjective process. Common words from the marina manager's mouth, "Sorry but your slip is reserved by a long-standing tenant who returns each year and he'll be arriving on Monday."

You won't find terms in your marina tenant agreement that give you the final word over the manager.

CHAPTER 3

Marina and Pier Characteristics

M arinas have a common purpose of providing dockage for vessels but they differ in numerous ways as discussed herein. The general configuration is typically based upon access to the sea or adjacent water body, with natural embayments, river mouths and Harbors of Refuge providing the earliest harbors in the U.S. as they required no dredging or channel clearing. As dredging techniques became more efficient via improved technologies, harbors and marinas sprung up in numerous coastal geographies, lakes and rivers, driven by the need for dockage for the local, growing populace. Likewise, commercial marine terminals were constructed with projected economic return.

If business potential looked favorable, often the only opposition to construction of new marinas was from environmental groups (protection of natural resources) and state/federal regulatory agencies (resource and pollution concerns). Although construction of new harbors and marinas has slowed greatly during the past two decades due to increased regulatory tightening, new facilities still arise in regions where the financial investors can cope with the often arduous and expensive regulatory process.

Marina Size Categories

Marinas can be characterized in many ways such as number of slips, size of largest vessel accommodated, type of ownership, etc. For characterizations by size (number of berths) the following categories are commonly used:

Size characterization	
Very Large	> 750 berths
Large	250–749
Medium	100–249
Small	1-99

Interesting annual statistics on marinas in the U.S. are compiled by *Marina Dock Age*, a trade magazine in existence for over 25 years to serve the marina and boatyard industry (see marinadockage.com). Key results from respondents (primarily marinas) are given below for 2013:

Marina ownership	
Private	73%
Government	15%
Corporate	6%
Condominium	4%
Yacht Club	2%

Marina size	
Large or Very Large	33%
Medium	32%
Small	30%

Average boat length (ft) in marina	
20 – 40 ft	74%
41 – 60 ft	21%
> 80 ft	2%

Geographic region of marinas	
South	46%
Northeast	21%
West	18%
Mid-west	16%

Regardless of marina size, most facilities offer dockage for a variety of vessel lengths. As indicated by the 2013 survey results, three quarters of the slips at respondents' facilities were less than 40 feet, whereas only 2 percent were over 80 feet. A brief discussion of marina size characteristics is given below.

VERY SMALL MARINAS

The term 'marina' is a stretch for some of the smallest facilities that try to lure small-boat owners into their facility for a brief visit and overnight. For example, it's possible to drive down a coastal road in southern Florida and see a sign like Sunset Motel and Marina. A quick turn into the facility confirms that the owner's definition of a marina is a boat ramp and a single dock to tie up two small boats, less than 20 feet each. These inexpensive small-boat launching facilities are common and it's great they exist for people who can't afford a larger vessel but still greatly enjoy a day on the water.

Water depth is often a limiting factor at these facilities because dredging is certainly out of the question due to costs.

SMALL MARINAS

Small marinas are typically defined (among marina industry folks) as facilities that have berths for up to 100 vessels. A small-boat owner may not view such a facility as a small marina but compared to those at the top-end of the marina spectrum, they are small. Even at these small facilities, a range of slip lengths is normally provided but most in the range from 30 to 50 feet. Often, a few large boats can be accommodated at end-ties of the main docks.

Depending upon whether the general vicinity of the marina is affluent and supporting a prosperous retail industry, small marinas also can be relatively up-scale, catering to mid- and large-size vessels despite the small number of berths. For example, a marina can have few slips below 50 feet while mainly catering to vessels from 75 to 150 feet – still a small marina by definition but often very expensive.

LARGE MARINAS

Large marinas are often defined as those with 250 or more berths, but in some conversations only marinas having more than 1,000 berths are characterized as large. Interestingly, the 2013 *Marina Dock Age* results showed there are roughly the same number of small, medium and large marinas. It is however, likely that many small and medium size marinas did not respond to the survey, thus pushing the percentage for large marinas higher than if all U.S. marinas were included in the survey calculation.

Marina Types

Alternatively, marinas can be characterized independent of their size. For example, the quality of the facility, its boating community and facility ownership are other ways to categorize marinas. The 2013 *Marina Dock Age* results demonstrated that 73 percent of the marinas responding to their survey were private marinas whereas government municipalities owned 15 percent. Corporate ownership was much smaller (6 percent), as were condominium (4 percent) and yacht club (2 percent) ownerships.

Provided below are brief (subjective) descriptions of various marina types.

Fishing Boat Marinas

Some marinas' primary purpose is to provide access to excellent fishing grounds. Vessels that berth in these fishing centers can be either:

- Private boats (typically small) for recreational fishing

- Charter boats that can be hired to take people out fishing for a day, sometimes longer or

- Commercial fishing vessels. These marinas typically do not cater to live-aboard tenants and accordingly, on-shore facilities are limited to bathrooms and parking lots.

Some of these marinas, which can be either privately owned or municipal facilities, do have a limited number of slips for private boaters who enjoy non-fishing recreation on the water.

BOAT YARDS

For the purpose of this discussion, boat yards are defined as facilities with a sole purpose of conducting vessel repair and maintenance. If they have berths, it is only for temporary dockage while the vessel is awaiting or under repair.

YACHT CLUBS

These facilities are privately or Association owned, have restricted membership and typically are very well maintained. Most are small when defined by number of slips and the majority of yacht clubs cater to sailing vessels versus motor yachts. Marina guidelines of yacht clubs are available only to members, as are their rate structures. Note that yacht clubs exclude long-term berthing of vessels owned by persons who are not members. Transient (short-term) slips are sometimes available for active members of other yacht clubs.

MUNICIPAL MARINAS

Being publicly owned, these facilities typically have minimal amenities and cater to the average local boater. Maintaining a low price for leased slips is often highest priority for these marinas. Some are well operated with competent dockmasters, helpful maintenance staff and useful support vessels and equipment. Most municipal marinas offer a range of slip types but they typically don't cater to large vessels because their municipal charter is to provide berthing opportunities for the largest number of boats and/or the typical local populace.

Interestingly, some municipal marinas (e.g., Santa Barbara, California) have only Equity Ownership slips, with a very long waiting list.

Full Service Marinas

This designation is common jargon for facilities that offer full marina dockage and amenities plus boat yard services. They typically are privately owned, for-profit facilities

Private Marinas

These facilities are the most common in the U.S. and they span all facility sizes, quality of amenities and cost ranges. Private marinas typically accommodate a variety of vessel types but some cater to very specific boating markets depending upon the demographics of the local community.

Before moving on, the role of private marinas in the U.S. is so pivotal that it deserves discussion. As pointed out by Neil Ross in multiple articles of *Marina Dock Age* magazine, the history of U.S. marinas was mostly founded after World War II when financial security was reestablished on a family basis. Automobiles were becoming commonplace and household funds sometimes arose for luxuries such as small boats. With market growth, along came the development of outboard motors and boat trailers. Weekend boating trips were within the grasp of middle class families.

As the boating population was expanding rapidly, so were opportunities to develop small marinas, especially in the absence of today's federal and local regulations against commercial development along the shoreline. Many Mom and Pop marinas sprouted up in the 1950s and '60s, with strong family business opportunities for their offspring. Today, many private marinas are still multi-generational ownerships, now with Generation Y (25- to 35-year-old) marina operators who are very computer savvy. The unsophisticated marinas of the past have now transformed into efficient, web-friendly, environmentally responsible facilities. If they didn't make this transition, they're not around today.

Congratulations to those private marinas that have become financially viable despite the challenges that come from many directions including: environmental regulations, taxation, insurance costs, customer awareness and stiff competition, often from large conglomerates with deep financial backing and ability for ownership of multiple marinas. Have respect for private marinas, especially those with long histories and a commitment to continue improving for its customers. They know their business.

RESORT MARINAS

These marinas are typically the most luxurious and often the most expensive. Most resort marinas are very small (less than 50 slips) while some can

accommodate over 500 vessels. What they all have in common are extraordinary on-shore amenities that are maintained to a high standard of quality for the resort guests or condominium residents.

Many resort marinas offer only transient (short-term) slips for guests whereas long-term lease and live-aboard status are found at very few resort marinas. If found, this type of on-board living can be outstanding.

MEGA-YACHT MARINAS

A small number of private marinas, typically located in metropolitan areas, cater to very large mega-yachts that can range from 100 to 400 feet in length. These expensive facilities typically have high security for obvious reasons, so inspection is difficult unless you can prove that you're a viable applicant. Note that some of these mega-yacht facilities have very few berths. Some have fewer than 20, so they would be categorized as small marinas despite the large size of their vessels.

Floating Yacht Dealerships

Boaters should be aware that other types of marinas exist solely for commercial enterprise. For example, some marinas operate as floating showrooms for vessels of one or more manufacturers. These typically do not lease slips to individual boat owners.

Dry Storage Marinas

Dry Storage Marinas are also called Dry-Dock Marinas, Rack Storage and Rackominiums. This type of facility has become popular around the country, mostly for small boats in saltwater and freshwater areas. Dry storage marinas are very economical because most have only a narrow channel with adequate depth for a boat to approach and depart from the facility. In-water boats do not tie up at the facility  because slips are typically absent altogether. Adjacent to the waterway is a boat ramp, a parking lot and one or more large, very tall utility-type buildings for dry storage of boats. Boats are lifted to and from its pre-assigned storage rack within the building. Racks can be stacked three or nine boats high depending upon the height of the building. Large forklifts are commonly used for stacking boats but many large storage buildings are equipped with an overhead railway for movement and stacking.

The advantages of on-land storage for small boats include the following:

- Good (possibly covered) protection from weather and storms while the boats are not in use. Possible reduction in boat insurance.

- Dry-hull storage that prevents galvanic corrosion and algae growth on vessel hulls.

- Prevention of minor vandalism, because boats are typically placed in racks that are 10 to 30 feet above the ground.

- Lower price than in-water slips.

- Options for regular maintenance and engine running by facility personnel to keep the boat and motors ready for use.

- Quick access and ease for the infrequent boater, because he/she can call ahead and their boat will be in the water running when they arrive.

DOCKOMINIUMS

This type of marina arrangement is often called equity slip ownership. Like a land-based condominium housing unit, the owner pays for asset (slip) ownership under terms of a contract but the physical property remains part of an overriding association that governs terms of use, facility maintenance, monthly facility usage costs, etc. If a boat owner likes a facility and intends to keep his/her vessel there for the long-term, an equity ownership contract (if offered) may prove advantageous over standard monthly or short-term slip lease. Recognize, however, that the term ownership is not exactly true under such contacts. Upon termination of the contract, the boat owner cannot gain any financial appreciation as would be the case for ownership/ sale of real estate property. Thus it should not be viewed as a good investment of financial capital; it may only be a way to keep slip costs from escalating over a long-term lease period.

Clean Marina Program

 With widespread concern about environmental health and clean oceans, the U.S. boating public and marinas nationwide have an opportunity to improve the health of our ecosystems and waterways by reducing pollutant contributions.

Starting in the early 1990s, the Environmental Protection Agency (EPA) implemented the Clean Vessel Act with financial grants to coastal and inland states for sewage pump-out stations and waste reception facilities that recreational boaters could use for disposal. Subsequently, the Clean Marina Program (CMP) was developed as a training, self-review and recognition program for marinas, boatyards and boaters. The program's primary purpose is to educate participants about environmental impacts of the marine industry and recreational activities. The CMP is run by individual states. The states are best positioned to establish regulations to address their local environmental and health concerns. States administer the program, while also remaining in compliance with federal regulations.

Voluntary and incentive-based, the CMP encourages marina operators and boaters to practice environmentally sound operating and maintenance procedures, including: proper waste disposal at marinas; regular boat engine inspection; and less discharge from boats of all types and sizes. The goal is to protect the marine environment as well as give qualifying marinas an economic competitive advantage.

Marinas that have committed to the CMP can gain from the following:

- Improved water quality and habitat for local marine life

- A clean, attractive appearance for boaters

- Reduced risk of liability and fines for violations of environmental regulations

- Financial Grant opportunities for the marina

- Recognition as an official Clean Marina and associated advertising advantages

The CMP varies by state yet is everywhere a public-private partnership between marina operators, the state and several federal agencies including NOAA and the EPA.

When boaters are evaluating a marina, they should inquire whether the facility has officially been designated as a Clean Marina and continues to implement Best Management Practices as specified by the state. If a marina is certified, they should be congratulated for doing their part to improve the marine environment at their personal (albeit business) expense.

Further details on the program can be obtained at the following websites and via local NOAA Sea Grant offices in their respective state:

EPA's Clean Marina Program
www.epa.gov/p2/pubs/casestudies/cleanmarina.htm

NOAA's Clean Marina Program
www.noaa.gov/features/resources_0509/marina.html

Slip Size and Characteristics

During your evaluation of a marina, it's best to find one that has a considerable number of slips to accommodate your specific vessel size. This will yield options for slip location that governs your boating neighbors, exposure to weather and seas, distance from the shore, parking, noise and other important factors. During your visit, walk the docks to view available slips, consider various pros and cons of different locations within the marina and most importantly, talk to existing tenants about which slips they view as optimum. Local knowledge is invaluable, as you'll hear throughout this guidebook.

Typically, marinas require tenants to lease a slip that is equal to or longer than the overall length of the vessel, inclusive of pulpit or bowsprit (fore) and swim platform or overhang (aft). They normally disallow vessels to extend more than 3 to 5 feet beyond the end of the slip or adjacent pilings so that the vessel does not interfere with vessel traffic in the adjacent channel or turning area (fairway) behind the slip. Boaters can usually lease a slip that is larger than their vessel unless large incoming vessels will require the slip. Oversized slips can be advantageous if you wish to pay the premium.

SINGLE SLIPS

Single Slips are those with a finger pier on each side of the docked vessel. These are very convenient because they allow boarding from either side of the vessel. Even more significant is that single slips are easiest for a novice captain to enter, given the 'bumpers' on each side of his inbound craft. However, vessel beam is often the deciding factor for tenants who wish to lease a single slip as sometimes the vessel's beam is too wide for a specific slip. This is frequently the case for catamarans (sail or power) that often have beams in the range of 20 to 30 feet.

There are, however, some disadvantages of single slips related to in-water storage of a vessel's dinghy. If there is sufficient room at the 'head' of the slip (closest to the main dock) a dinghy can be tied there but then it's trapped until the main vessel exits. Some (but not all) marinas allow dinghies to be tied aft of the main vessel (i.e., in the fairway) but only if they don't extend too far out and thus become a hazard to vessels navigating in marina channels. Note that risk of theft increases in that configuration too, versus the 'captive' type docking situation for a dinghy.

> ### • IMPORTANT REMINDER •
>
> *Finger piers can sometimes extend only half the length of a slip, which can be a major problem if the boarding location on a vessel is past the end of the finger pier. When you are viewing a marina and looking at potential slips for your vessel, be sure to note whether all finger piers extend the full length of the slip.*

DOUBLE SLIPS

Double slips are marina spaces where two boats dock side-by-side without a finger pier between. Boarding of each boat is accomplished on a single side of each hull. Double slips are common in many marinas because the absence of a finger pier translates into more tenant boats per length of

the main dock and thus more money for the marina owner. For new boaters, double slips can be a significant challenge when entering while the neighbor boat is berthed in its slip. Efficient fender placement is a necessity on both boats to prevent hull damage.

The close proximity of neighboring boats in double slips also can result in noise issues so try to assess your future neighbor if you are considering a long-term lease. Like in real estate situations, value is all about 'location' and there's nothing worse than being berthed next to a derelict, unpainted, near-sinking boat with barking dogs, frequent parties, loud music, cigar smokers, etc.

Marinas that offer single and double slips of the same length should provide lower rates for double slips, as they are less convenient for boaters. Try to negotiate a lower rate if you are forced to lease a double slip versus an available single slip, but if the marina is nearly full it's unlikely there will be any wiggle room on rates.

Some marinas have one or more center pilings situated in the middle of the larger double slips to facilitate better positioning of dock lines of each vessel. These pilings are very helpful to boaters. Such pilings are placed only in very wide double slips, which translates into more space between vessels for reduced hull damage, more privacy and potentially, more room for in-water dinghy storage between the main vessels. Thus, wide Double Slips can be more advantageous than Single Slips to some boat owners.

A final comment on single and double slips pertains to the turning area adjacent to the slip. Note that main docks are situated to provide a small space for turning of small vessels as they enter or depart from small slips. This turning area is considered a traffic lane and referred to as the 'fairway' by marina designers. For larger vessels berthed in large slips, the fairway is wider to facilitate the vessel having to turn ninety degrees upon entry and departure (unlike for side-tie slips). For large vessels and mega-yachts, bow and stern thrusters can make the turning job much easier but fairways must still be quite large to accommodate the considerable vessel size.

All novice boaters should carefully (with assistance from an experienced boater) assess the size of the turning area for the slip he/she intends to lease.

Heed this warning because there are some marinas that are designed so poorly that a novice boater cannot safely maneuver his vessel into or out of the slip if there is any wind or current. Not a good situation to discover after you have signed a tenant agreement. In such cases, boaters may have to lease a different slip that is considerably longer than their vessel (and with a wider turning area) so that safe docking can be accomplished under all conditions.

SIDE-TIE SLIPS

Side-tie slips offer dockage adjacent to a long pier with 'open water' on the outboard side of the hull. Upon first glance, this seems terrific for docking because it doesn't require bow- or stern-approach to a narrow slip but it can pose other challenges for the boat operator.

Typically the boater with a side-tie slip can choose whether to dock his/her boat with the port or starboard side adjacent to the dock. This is convenient for boats that are configured for boarding at a position well forward of the stern but for transom-boarding vessels; side-tie slips do not work.

The biggest challenge for docking at side-tie slips is during crosswinds that blow from the dock toward open water; similarly, when currents are tending perpendicular and away from the dock either due to tidal currents or river flow. Under these conditions, the vessel is pushed away from the side-tie slip and docking requires either bow/stern thrusters or significant skill with dock lines while using considerable vessel power (not recommended for novices). As a final comment to beginners: don't sign up for a side-tie slip if crosswinds or currents are frequent, even though the slip may look charming and spacious.

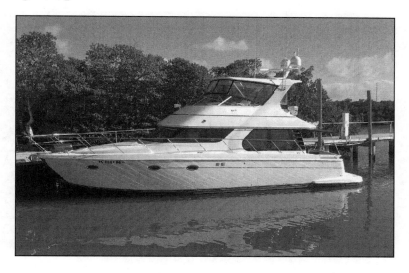

END-TIE SLIPS

End-tie slips, often called T-docks, are side-tie slips located at the end position on long docks. In end-tie slips, vessels dock port- or starboard- side to. Access to open water is certainly easiest from these slips. Because vessel length is typically not a limitation, these slips are reserved for relatively large vessels and consequently have high rates. In some marinas end-tie slips are very long and multiple vessels can tie up end-to-end.

Fixed Versus Floating Docks

In the coastal U.S. there are regions that experience tidal ranges (the vertical distance from low water to high) as low as one foot while other regions can encounter 15 feet of range between high and low water, especially at times of Spring tides. Regions with small vertical ranges easily accommodate vessel berthing via fixed docks, similar to those constructed in lakes that are absent of tides, but such regions represent a small percentage of coastal marinas nationally.

It is important that a boater learn the different dock types because they have a major impact on many day-to-day factors of marina life, including:

- Ease of vessel access by passengers

- Loading of supplies and equipment

- Difficulty of fueling, water fill and sewage pump-out

- Tending of power cords and other cabling

- Fenders and most importantly

- Dock lines

FIXED DOCKS

Fixed Docks include docks adjacent to land as well as docks extending outward from shore and some with attached, perpendicular finger piers. All can be 'fixed' in the vertical, typically built on wood pilings or attached to steel sheet-piles that are firmly jetted into the bottom. Only the vessel rises with changes in the water level; everything else stays fixed in the vertical. In practical terms, the dock lines of the berthed vessel must be long enough to accommodate vessel rise during high tide and subsequent descent at low water. Additional vertical range must be considered if river stage, storm surge or other factors can affect water level changes in the marina. If lines get prohibitively taut during water level changes,  extensive damage to the vessel and/or docks can occur. Beware that all marina tenant agreements stipulate that if damage to docks occurs due to negligent rigging of a boat's dock lines, the liability and cost of repairs to the dock is borne by the vessel owner. Thus, vessel damage is only half of the problem for the owner.

In common practice, when fixed docks are used in regions of minimal tidal range, the main issue for boat owners is minor inconvenience during loading. Loading ramps and dockside steps can normally be used to facilitate reasonable access with minimal angst. Fendering and providing appropriate slack for dock lines are skills that can be learned in a few days of on-site observations of tidal variability — certainly not 'rocket science'.

• IMPORTANT REMINDER •

Know your local tides and predict when your largest ranges will occur so you can attend to your dock lines wisely.

FLOATING DOCKS

Floating Docks are standard equipment in most marinas around the U.S. and occur in all types of configurations and construction materials. The simplest configuration is for a vessel to be attached to a floating pier that rises and falls freely with tidal fluctuations and other water level changes. The gunnel of the boat remains in roughly the same vertical position relative to the top of the floating pier, in contrast to fixed piers where the vessel is always moving vertically relative to the pier.

A simple floating pier can be connected to shore or stationary structure via a loading ramp that changes its angle from the horizontal with changes in water level. Floating piers can be solitary or connected (rafted) in long arrays of attached piers but all must be attached (loosely) to some type of fixed structure to prevent lateral movement.

The basic configuration of floating pier has a few metal or chain 'bales' on each end of the pier that slide up and down adjacent vertical poles or pilings. Other floating pier configurations are tethered by line or chain to seabed anchors or structures so the pier is free to rise and fall vertically while having limited horizontal range.

Boaters normally prefer floating piers because they require a minimal vertical climb into their vessels from the pier, even if the ramp from the pier to shore is steep during very low water levels. More significantly, dock lines can be attached tighter and more reliably to floating piers in contrast to the considerable skill required to estimate sufficient slack on all lines for vessels attached to fixed piers. The same goes for tending of all hoses and cables required between the vessel and the dock. Trust me — floating docks are much easier than fixed docks for safely berthing your vessel in a marina, especially if you plan to be away from the vessel for significant periods of 'worry' time.

Dock Materials

The physical characteristics of your dock's horizontal surface are important and should be a consideration when comparing marinas. Old and poorly maintained facilities typically have painted planks or plywood decks that can be weak, inferior surfaces with uneven seams. Other old piers may be constructed from a plywood base, upon which a grid of iron reinforcing rods is placed, then a top layer of concrete four to eight inches thick is poured over the grid to provide a durable surface with inner strength. These are good, relatively inexpensive deck surfaces that can be painted and made with non-slip texture but

their useful life is often limited to 5 to 10 years before cracking begins; somewhat longer in mild climates.

Similarly, conventional wooden planks provide inexpensive decking but even marine-grade, pressure-treated lumber has adverse characteristics such as splintering, warping, release of toxic chemicals, etc.

Paintable aluminum planks and decking are another alternative with good resistance to environmental factors but cost of these products is significant.

If cost is not a factor, teak and Brazilian hardwood planks can be used for excellent decking that is water resistant, mildew retardant and appealing to the eye but such materials are uncommon at most marinas.

Bellingham Marine Industries offers two concrete floating dock systems with advantages of strength, durability, proven performance, non-flammable and non-skid surfaces, wave resistance, protection for boats, corrosion resistance and environmental compatibility. While these dock systems are relatively heavy and expensive compared to more basic dock components, they also offer great stability, endurance and resistance to mechanical fatigue. Some of the largest marinas in the U.S. have reconfigured with concrete floating docks with good satisfaction.

During recent years with growing public pressure for use of environmentally safe 'green' materials, a variety of renewable and recyclable decking products have become commercially available at moderately affordable prices. Many new marinas as well as others upgrading their docks are choosing these composite products for dock surfaces. It's not surprising because these decking products offer low maintenance, non-skid surfaces, color options, no splin-

tering, coolness and fast drying capabilities, non-combustible and non-staining material, etc.

These new deck products can be composites of resin and organic materials (e.g., sawdust or husks from rice grains) or totally vinyl/resin based. Leading products have trade names of Trex, Evolve, Azek PVC and others.

There have been recent cases where composite decks have posed significant drawbacks. In addition to becoming very hot in midday sun, some composite materials can transfer significant static electricity charges to someone walking on the dock. When the boater touches the metal rail of a vessel or ramp, electricity can be discharged to the unsuspecting person with adverse consequences. As environmental conditions will certainly affect the likelihood of this situation, this topic warrants further investigation.

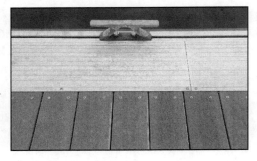

If your preferred marina has composite dock surfaces, that is a major benefit. If not, marina management personnel may be defensive about their old docks versus their competition and consequently inform you that all dock surfaces will be replaced with new materials in a year or two. Great news (if it's true) but you should check their marina tenant agreement to ensure that your dockage fees cannot rise more than a small and reasonable percentage each year. It is not uncommon for marinas to increase their slip lease rates considerably after they make significant upgrades to their facilities such as new docks, pump-out systems, parking facilities, laundry, pool, etc.

Control Depths and Channel Draft

This simple topic can be critically important. Control Depth is the term used to specify the minimum depth of a waterway (at low water or minimum stage of a river) for purposes of vessel passage. For example, when a dredge has completed the deepening of a channel or harbor, it must assure that the water is everywhere (at least) as deep as the specified Control Depth under the vertical conditions specified (e.g., tidal datum or river stage).

Relating to Control Depths, there are two factors to consider when evaluating marina suitability for your vessel:

1. The water depth in your targeted marina slip should be at least 3 feet deeper than your vessel's draft at the time of lower low water in saltwater regions (e.g., at the time of a 'Spring tide').

2. Channels between your marina and your intended cruising areas must have sufficient and reliable draft to provide safe access and navigation. Those that provide adequate passage only during high tide should be avoided. Similarly, those harbors or channels that are subject to natural shoaling and are not routinely dredged should definitely be avoided because your vessel may be at risk of grounding each time you venture out of the marina.

When you are speaking with the management of a marina or with their dockmaster about potential dockage, be sure to inquire about depths within their facility as well as within adjacent channels. If they demonstrate lack of confidence in water depths at their facility, leave immediately and search for another marina. If they are uncertain about channel depths in the harbor or its approaches, speak directly to the local harbormaster to get the real story.

Most importantly, marina tenant agreements (as you will read later) exclude the marina from all liability associated with water depths and vessel grounding.

• CHAPTER 4 •
Marina Essentials

T his chapter addresses key elements that contribute to safe, efficient, comfortable and enjoyable boating experiences at your marina.

Boating Community

A significant part of the boating experience is the camaraderie that develops among fellow boaters at a marina. I often tell my non-boating friends that marinas are a wonderful place to meet fascinating people from all sorts of backgrounds who dare choose the sea-going lifestyle, for recreation and sometimes to live aboard as their primary residence. Despite the diversity of personal backgrounds and prior lives, most boaters have terrific personal energy and amazing stories to tell about places visited, favorite experiences and challenging adventures on the 'briny', lake or river.

Another element of marina life in coastal areas is that people and boats are constantly moving around. Not all, but many boats in coastal marinas stay for a week or a few months then move on to their next destinations. Some return to the same marina each year as part of their seasonal cruising circuit and it's wonderful reacquainting, hearing their stories and planning joint adventures. Lasting friendships often develop and people cruise together for companionship as well as safety gained from multiple vessels.

Boaters are sometimes saddened to hear that old captain Bill and his wife Alice bought the farm, which is boaters' jargon for buying a home on land and selling their boat. Living in one place forever after is doom for many avid cruisers, especially knowing that Bill and Alice will have a limited number of neighbors who are probably less adventurous than all their past, fearless mariner friends.

When you're searching for your optimum marina, of course you're looking for a fine place to keep your boat but you mustn't overlook the importance of selecting the right boating community for you. Ideally, you'll find like-minded people with similar interests, energy levels and social graces.

Decide which of these boating communities would best suit you:

- **'Party town'** with lots of dock life and music

- **'Mega-yacht haven'** where huge, expensive vessels shine brightly

- **'Fishing frenzy'** with active boats and often a lively drinking crew

- **'Sailor's stop'** where sailboats congregate before moving on

- **'Cruisers port'** where cruisers spend a while before they move too

- **'Family friendly'** where lots of children enjoy all that boating has to offer

- **'Pet friendly'** where boat owners care greatly about their four-footed best friends

- **'Retired live-aboards'** - a quiet community enjoying the easy life

Look carefully when visiting marinas and try to make your visits on busy weekends so you can feel the pulse of the local boating community. It's essential and you'll thank yourself for making the right choice for many years to come.

Shore Power

Reliable AC (alternating current) electrical power is required by most vessels while docked in their marina slip. Depending upon the size and complexity of your vessel's electrical needs, power may be required for any or all of the following uses: bilge pumps, battery chargers, lights, refrigeration appliances, security systems, air conditioning units, dehumidifiers, fuel polish-

ing systems, etc. Vessels may require 115 or 230 volts AC and amperages of 30, 50 or 100. It is essential that your marina provide uninterrupted AC power to match your voltage and amperage requirements.

It's strongly recommended that you walk the docks and speak with existing marina tenants to determine first-hand whether marina shore power is reliable, maintains a near-constant voltage and is rarely shut off, even for short durations. Any major deficiencies in shore power could put your vessel in significant jeopardy when unattended. It's also wise to place an AC-powered light in full view from the dock so that owners of neighboring vessels could contact you if your AC power appears to be off when you're away from the marina.

As you're assessing a slip that may be assigned for your vessel, be sure to determine where the shore power connector is located. The best case is having it situated immediately adjacent to your slip but oftentimes it's located as much as 50 feet away. It's your responsibility to provide the AC cable from the shore connector to your vessel and marinas will not provide extension cables, except for purchase.

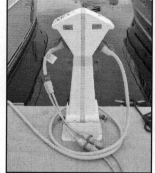

The next step is to locate the external shore power connector on your vessel (port or starboard side, bow or stern?). Start measuring to determine whether you have sufficient length of cable to make shore connection.

If you are new to boating and your yacht has an automatic, electrically powered, below-deck system for coiling your power cable (e.g., a Cable Master system), extend it fully to determine its length capability. In most cases, your on-board cable can extend sufficiently to reach the shore connector if your vessel is berthed 'stern-to' in the slip. Conversely, your vessel may need to be 'bow-in' for your cable to reach the connector. Beware that without an extension cable; your existing power configuration will most likely dictate how your vessel will be oriented in the slip. It's a terrible fate when your cockpit can't face the sunset at cocktail hour.

If you decide to purchase a shore-power extension cable to allow freedom to berth your vessel either way, consult with a marine electrician or someone with knowledge of which cable to purchase for interfacing with your power system and amperage needs. Selection of the proper cable is not as simple as the novice might think. For example, cables must be marine-rated with corrosion resistant materials and oil-resistant, UV-stabilized jackets. They also must have correct voltage and

amperage ratings; the correct watertight, molded end-connectors for your usage; and heavy gauge stranded wire with four conductors rather than three for proper grounding of high-amperage cables. Sound confusing? It is. Marine components are special so ask an expert before you purchase the wrong cable and waste $500 to $800.

Fresh Water

A continuous source of potable fresh water should be provided on the pier adjacent to (i.e., within 50 feet of) your vessel for onboard dishwashing, showers, exterior hull washing, etc. For larger vessels with onboard toilets (heads), some use fresh water rather than salt water for their waste delivery to the onboard waste holding tanks.

The pier's water supply should have a spigot with operable shut-off valve and a male garden hose fitting to accept your connection hose. If any deficiencies are encountered, contact marina maintenance personnel for repairs rather than do it yourself otherwise you may be liable for any leaks or associated damages thereafter.

Vessels have onboard freshwater tanks that vary greatly in capacity but are proportional to the size of the vessel (e.g., 30 gal for a small vessel; 150 gal for a 50-ft vessel; 500 gal for an 80-ft vessel, etc.). Typically, the onboard tank is filled by a portable hose then disconnected from the water source on the dock. In some cases however (primarily in live-aboard situations) the owner may shut off the water valve but leave the fill hose connected to his onboard tank. This is the easiest way to sink a berthed vessel because failure of any shut-off valve, either on the dock or aboard your vessel may result in constant flow into your boat that is often unnoticed until it's too late.

Normally, the fresh water provided by the marina is city water that has consistent high quality and is adequate for cooking, drinking and bathing. It is however, wise to periodically check the water to see if it contains unwanted particulates or odd coloration which may be due to long residence times of the water in the plumbing lines of marinas. Before filling your vessel, run the water for a minute or longer to ensure that any contaminated water in your hose or nearby pipes is discarded. If other boats have not filled lately, it is possible that your water could have been sitting idle in pipes and hoses for many days or longer and/or in very warm temperatures that could result in particulates dislodging from the inside of old pipes.

Water purification systems of various sophistication and expense can be purchased for filtration of incoming fresh water. Small units can be set up on the dock adjacent to the marina's fresh water spigot for basic filtering. Larger purification systems can be installed aboard large vessels to achieve much higher levels of water purity.

Many boat owners use the marina's city water for all onboard functions except for drinking, as bottled spring water can be brought aboard quite simply and economically.

Note that if the quality of the freshwater from your onboard tank is poor or contains an offensive odor, the problem may reside in your tank rather than from the shore-side source. For minor mold problems in tanks, a small amount of household bleach can be added to a full tank for simple cleaning. Do this before you head out to sea so the bleach is mixed by the rolling action of the vessel. If this does not solve the problem, the tank should be opened and professionally cleaned.

Sanitary Pump-Out

Federal regulations specify that sewage (human wastes) generated aboard your vessel must not be discharged into rivers, harbors or coastal waters. In the Great Lakes, this regulation also includes water from bathing and galley wastes. Consequently, the majority of vessels operating in U.S. waters are equipped with below-deck waste holding tanks, which are classified by the U.S. Coast Guard as Type III Marine Sanitation Devices (MSDs). See the Glossary for the website link to official MSD regulations.

STANDARD PROCEDURES IN HARBORS

Boaters are required to keep all 'black-water' valves positioned so that toilet discharges flow directly into the onboard waste tank, rather than allowing overboard discharge. Some marinas that accommodate transient boats have special procedures to prevent accidental discharge of sewage waste into their harbors. In such cases, marina personnel attach a lock to the two-position (overboard or tank) valve for black water so that it can only flow into the waste tank while the vessel resides in the harbor. Dye can also be added to the waste tank to reveal if the vessel discharges waste into the harbor. Major fines are levied for violators of waste discharge guidelines so beware.

MARINA PUMP-OUT FACILITIES

Most new marinas have built-in sewage plumbing on all docks to facilitate connection to a shore-based pumping station for convenient removal of sewage from vessel holding tanks of tenant vessels. The optimum situation is a pump-out connection at each slip. Otherwise, a long (i.e., 70-foot) flexible hose coiled on a wheeled cart is moved to the vessel for pump-out services. One end of the hose is attached securely to a special sewage-waste spigot on the dock while the other end is inserted into the sewage pump-out line of the vessel, typically located on deck. Note that the diameter of your sewage discharge cap/line may differ from the diameter of the fitting on the waste pumping hose. Be sure to resolve this issue of size compatibility when you arrive in the marina because it may be necessary to purchase an adapter for connection to the marina's pump-out hose.

When both ends of the pump-out hose are securely connected, the operator activates the shore-based pump and sewage is then vacuum-pumped out of the vessel. Some marinas provide staff for pumping while other facilities allow tenants to pump out their waste tank as necessary. The latter case is best because of schedule flexibility but either is certainly better than other means. Normally, the marina pump-out service is included in the slip fee rather than charged per pump-out event.

MOBILE PUMP-OUT SERVICES

If the marina facility does not offer dockside pump-out services, some locations have commercial sewage removal companies with on-road tank trucks or waste pumping vessels that can visit your vessel for pump-out. This service can be quite expensive, anywhere from $25 to $100 depending upon the size of your vessel's waste holding tank.

In recent years, some states and many municipalities nationwide have chosen to establish free pump-out facilities and services to encourage boater use. This certainly will improve water quality in areas where boaters discharge illegally rather than pay the local pump-out fee.

PUMP-OUT DOCKS

Some cities provide a pump-out station on a city dock within the harbor to encourage responsible discharge of sewage waste. Normally this is free but quite often the systems are broken or unreliable because of excessive use and substandard maintenance. The fitting on the pump-out hose may not fit your discharge port so consider having an adaptor aboard your vessel. Also, do not assume the city pump-out station is working when your tank is full. Have a backup plan identified.

AT-SEA DISCHARGE

Only when vessels are more than 3 nautical miles offshore in federal coastal waters is at-sea discharge of sewage waste permitted. Discharge from the onboard sewage waste tank aboard a vessel is conducted using a special macerator pump that chops any solid wastes into small particulates while passing through the pump. Discharge into the sea is via a through-hull port beneath the water line of the vessel such that the waste slurry may be difficult to view unless the vessel is stationary. Guidelines on waste discharge at sea are given earlier in this section.

WARNING

Vacuum pressure of pump-out systems can vary considerably. Everyone complains when the suction is so weak that it takes a long time to pump out their waste tank. This also can occur when the air vent line from the waste tank becomes temporarily clogged. At other times, the vacuum system can drop its prime and the nozzle will need to be submerged in the harbor water to reestablish suction. These are not problems – just inconveniences.

Real problems arise during pump-out if the suction of the system is too strong. Under extreme circumstances, it's possible for a weak waste tank to implode – this is a big problem. In other cases, excessive suction can cause any of the numerous waste hoses and hose clamps of the waste system to begin leaking. A third problem that can arise is a rupture of the check valve in the hose that leads from the waste tank to the macerator pump that pumps wastewater overboard, when operated. If the valve or pump is damaged by the excessive suction of pump-out, and the through-hull valve is left open, then seawater is free to fill the waste tank – another big problem. This may start slowly but if the level indicator of the waste tank continues to rise without use of the onboard heads (toilets), suspect that the valve and/or pump have been damaged. Test these components and get the problem fixed soon.

Vessel Fuel

This discussion pertains to relatively large vessels that remain in the water either year-round or an entire boating season and cannot be trailered to a fueling station. Best options for purchasing vessel fuel are dependent upon the volume you intend to purchase. Always try to negotiate, especially if you intend to purchase hundreds of gallons at one time. For purchases of one thousand gallons or more, you should be able to negotiate a price that is much less than the small-volume (retail) price. Remember however, that fuel quality must be your highest priority, over price.

FUEL DOCKS

Some harbors offer only a single authorized fuel dock; this is certainly the worst case for boaters with regard to price as there is no competition. Such limitations on harbor fuel docks are greatest in California where environmental considerations supersede boaters' price concerns. Similarly, at most California marinas, boaters are not able to transport fuel in jerry cans due to concern about small fuel spills during fueling of vessels.

In comparison to this worst case, many harbors in other states have multiple fuel companies with their own docks and competition keeps fuel prices reasonable. However, don't be surprised when you see that all fuel dock prices are much higher than those at roadside fueling stations, regardless of gas or diesel. This is primarily a case of boaters being a 'captive audience' in the eyes of the dockside fuel retailers who often set prices high. Yes, they have additional challenges with delivery inconveniences, difficult fuel storage issues, etc., but when their prices are $1 to $2 per gallon higher than roadside filling stations, the boater has to wonder if it's price gouging.

Note that if your marina has a fuel dock, tenants are often given a discount from quoted retail prices. Ask for a discount even if you don't see one advertised.

FUEL TANK TRUCKS

Some cities and marinas allow fuel deliveries to vessels by truck or via floating fuel barges (for very large deliveries). This is the best-case scenario because it increases competition with suppliers at local fuel docks. It is recommended that boat owners contact the various suppliers to determine the source of their fuel, price per gallon for various quantities, any filtration capabilities on their trucks (a positive) and whether they add biocides or fuel stabilizers in the case of diesel fuel (very important).

When obtaining phone quotes per gallon, verify that they include all fees because you'll be peeved later if they add federal tax, city tax and a marina surcharge for delivery at their facility (totaling another fifty cents per gallon, often). In contrast, prices at fuel docks normally are quoted with all fees included but verify this.

Also before purchasing fuel, it is strongly recommended that you speak with other boaters to determine whether any suppliers have provided poor quality fuel to vessels. This happens and it can cost the boat owner thousands of dollars for various remedies, including pumping all of the contaminated fuel from the below-deck tanks, paying for disposal of this hazardous waste, professionally steam cleaning the tanks and repairing any damage to engines caused by use of the bad fuel.

The most common problems with bad fuel on vessels are:

- Water in the fuel

- Particulates in the fuel

- Algae accumulation in the fuel tanks and

- Chemical contamination and breakdown of the fuel that has been stored onboard for many months.

Most major cities have laboratories where fuels can be tested chemically so if you suspect a problem with purchased fuel, have a laboratory analysis conducted on a sample of your fuel so you can 'negotiate' with the supplier; hopefully having them pay for removal of the bad fuel and reimbursing you for the initial purchase.

Fuel 'polishing' systems and other techniques have been developed in recent years to clean and condition fuel that resides in vessel tanks for more than a couple months but this topic is beyond the scope of this marina guidebook. Note that these systems are typically designed to remove water and particulates from the fuel but they do nothing to resolve chemical problems with fuel.

Shower and Bathroom Facilities

For boaters who do not have adequate bathing facilities aboard their vessel, marina shower facilities are an important aspect of life quality. During your on-site evaluation of a new marina, view the shower and changing facilities for size, cleanliness and hours of accessibility. Are the facilities stark or preferably, like a with towels and bathing products provided, as found at some high-end resort marinas? More importantly, during morning 'rush hour' is there a sufficient number of shower stalls to prevent a waiting line with frustrated, towel-holding tenants. Years ago I had been a tenant at a medium-sized marina were many of the boaters were still gainfully employed five days per week. Each morning the guys had to wait in line up to 30 minutes for a shower stall to become available. Two operational showers certainly were insufficient.

The number and cleanliness of the marina's bathroom facilities for tenants also are important issues for boaters, likely under differing circumstances. For example, some boats do not have adequate toilets on board, others may have their waste tank(s) full, while an unlucky few may have inoperable sanitary systems. Regardless of the size of your vessel, it's likely that you'll be using the marina's bathroom at some time or other. If your partner or guest is very particular about his/her 'sanitary facilities' then you had better select a marina with clean, well-maintained bathroom facilities or you'll catch hell for sure.

Laundry Facilities

Similarly, most marinas are obligated to provide machines for clothes washing and drying. Because they're normally coin-operated machines, inquire at the marina office about self-  service machines for change – you'll need one for sure. If the marina has a good security program, only marina tenants may use the laundry facilities. Conversely, if the facility is open to the public, theft and damage to machines may become a significant deterrent to using the marina's laundry facility. Ask other tenants whether they have encountered any problems in the laundry area; if so, have your laundry done offsite.

Marina management personnel can normally provide a list of dry cleaning facilities and/or wash-and-fold laundries. Some businesses even provide free pick-up and drop-off at larger marinas so be sure to inquire about this helpful service.

Car Parking and Security

Marinas that are city-owned typically do not provide safe, secure parking for tenants' automobiles and trailers. Similarly, small privately owned marinas with minimal facilities rarely have secure parking. Vandalism can be a problem at these locations so ask boaters at those facilities what precautions they take to protect their vehicles when parked on-site, especially when cruising for a few days or longer.

Larger, privately maintained marinas normally have gated parking facilities, good lighting and security cameras around the facility to protect the property of tenants. Depending upon the neighborhood, these may provide sufficient protection for your vehicles. If, however, you plan to cruise away from your marina for an extended period of time (say weeks or months), investigate options for long-term storage rather than leave your vehicle unattended.

Some marinas (typically those associated with a condominium facility) offer garages for tenant lease for vehicle storage. Other less-robust facilities have securely locked parking lots for long-term storage, which certainly are better than leaving a car in a transient lot with significant risk of damage. The last option is to investigate local commercial facilities for long-term vehicle storage.

Tenant Pets

Marina tenant agreements often specify what types of domestic pets are permitted aboard berthed vessels. New boaters typically don't have much concern about this clause because they don't expect to see pets aboard vessels. A seagoing cat or dog may seem odd to some people but they're actually quite common among boaters.

The flexibility that marinas demonstrate with regard to their pet policy can vary greatly. For example, some marinas discourage pets and permit only a single small dog or cat aboard. They also can specify many types of mammals, birds, reptiles and other species that are disallowed. Fish seem to be permitted aboard vessels, not surprisingly.

In contrast, some marinas welcome pets aboard tenant vessels because they acknowledge pets can be a significant part of life for many boaters, especially some that live aboard permanently. While marinas have clearly defined pet policies, most are flexible and do not enforce the rules unless a tenant's pet causes a nuisance. Marinas are most lenient about pets of good tenants. Remember my early statement that cooperation can yield gains for the good tenant?

Having been a tenant in numerous marinas on the east and west coasts, I have seen many surprising pet situations — some of the most memorable are given below (each on single boats):

- Caged, loud birds

- Four cats

- Two very large dogs (one a Great Dane)

- An iguana

- A ferret

- Snakes

- A Service Dog for the disabled (for a blind man living aboard alone.)

- And on one sailboat: three dogs, two cats and a bird. The vessel should have been named "Ark".

It is surprising how well most dogs and some cats take to living aboard a boat. The excitement demonstrated by the dogs as they jump onto the dock for their twice-per-day 'runs' is wonderful. They have their time to play with fellow pets from other vessels but most walk slowly when returning to their floating homes, forlorn with the reality of more confinement. Cats don't care about shore-time nor socializing.

For tenants without pets, the marina situation is typically okay unless the dogs and birds on a neighboring vessel make excessive noise and their owners don't take action. The worst case is when dogs bark excessively when their masters are off the boat. Marina management should be notified of any recurring problems as everyone is entitled to quiet living.

• AUTHOR RECOMMENDATION •

If domestic pets are an important part of your life and you plan to have them aboard your vessel, it is very important that you assess a marina's 'attitude' toward pets on your first visit. Reading the tenant agreement should be step one but there are other things to assess during your walk around the marina facility, including:

- A dog park should be sufficient in size to accommodate many dogs, fenced and well maintained.

- Waste bags should be easily accessible at multiple locations around the marina facility; not just in the dog park.

- The marina should be environmentally responsible and pet friendly, taking care not to spray or distribute excess amounts of toxic chemicals that could harm tenant pets.

- Marina proximity to veterinary services is important too, but this is not a marina responsibility.

Also, if you hear from boaters that one vessel has many cats aboard, you probably don't want to be their neighbor. There have been instances when cats have left their home vessel to temporarily board a neighboring vessel to attend to bodily functions. This is not a good situation to return to after a week away from your vessel.

CHAPTER 5

Tides

All coastal boaters need a basic understanding of tides because they pose significant impacts on boating. With regard to marina life, tides are the primary process governing daily water level changes and associated currents. While tides are totally predictable at a given location, their characteristics vary greatly with location around the coastal U.S. as discussed below.

Tidal Effects on Water Level

Semi-diurnal tides are common in U.S. coastal waters and characterized by two highs and two lows daily. Driven by the gravitational pull from the moon and sun, they result in two simultaneous bulges on the ocean surface: one in the direction of the extra-planetary pull and the other on the opposite side of the earth. The gravitational pull from the moon is strongest due to its close proximity to the earth. Despite the massive size of the sun, its great distance from the earth causes its gravitational pull on our ocean to be only 46 percent of that from the moon.

The semi-diurnal (S-D) tide is a combination of the lunar tide with period 12.42 hours and the solar tide with period of 12 hours. This can result in varying heights of the two high-water (and two low-water) events during a single day; such variability are called inequalities to tidal enthusiasts.

Along the U.S. East Coast, tides are purely S-D, with no significant diurnal components. In Maine near the Canadian border, the S-D tide has a range of roughly 16 feet, partly due to its proximity to the Bay of Fundy in Nova Scotia, which sometimes experiences ranges approaching 30 feet on account of the coastline geometry that causes natural resonant amplification (increased vertical height) of the tide. With further distance to the south along the New England coastline, S-D tidal ranges decrease to 10 feet at Boston. South of Cape Cod in Massachusetts, S-D amplitudes are much less, ranging from 3 to 4 feet along the entire Atlantic coast between Nantucket and the Outer Banks of North Carolina. S-D amplitudes rise to near 5 feet along South Carolina and northeast Florida but drop again to 2 feet in southeast Florida and throughout the Florida Keys.

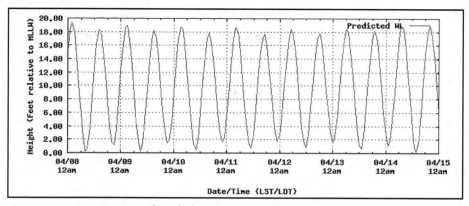

Eastport, Maine water level showing Semi-Diurnal tide over seven days. 20-ft tidal range with two highs each day.

Note that every two weeks, the moon and sun are in alignment, causing intensification of the gravitational pull and greater ranges (amplitudes) of the S-D tide. These events are called Spring tides (moon tides in some regions), with no connection to our climatological seasons. Relatively weaker S-D tides, called Neap tides, occur when the moon and sun are at 90 degrees to each other in relation to the earth's surface and the gravitational pulls are consequently misaligned.

Diurnal tides have a period of 24 hours, equivalent to our solar day and resulting in one high water and one low water event per day. Generally, the diurnal tide is substantially weaker than S-D tidal amplitudes because it results from two relatively minor factors: 1) the inclination of the Earth's rotational axis from the horizontal, orbital plane of the moon and 2) effects associated with the earth's revolution around the sun.

Along the East Coast of the U.S., diurnal tidal amplitudes are negligible so tides appear purely S-D. In direct contrast, S-D tides are negligible in the Gulf of Mexico such that diurnal tides dominate there, although they are weak. Along the entire coast of the Gulf of Mexico, tidal ranges are only 1 to 2 feet. Outflow from major rivers (e.g., Mobile, Mississippi and Rio Grande) certainly have major impacts on local water levels but their effects on hourly water level fluctuations are small except during storm events.

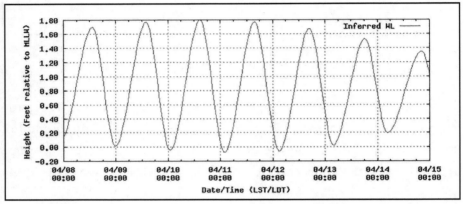

Biloxi, MS water level showing Diurnal tide over seven days.
2-ft tidal range with one high each day.

Mixed tides occur when both S-D and diurnal tides are significant at a specific location. Two highs may occur in a single day but they typically have different amplitudes; the same for amplitudes of low water. On some days there is only one high tide depending upon how the S-D and diurnal tidal amplitudes conflict and cancel each other. A single low-water event can occur on other days. Overall, water level records in regions of mixed tides are very irregular compared to the nearly sinusoidal shape of purely S-D records.

The entire West Coast of the U.S. is characterized by mixed tides, from the Mexican border to Canada and along the southern Alaska coast to the Aleutian Islands. Ranges of mixed tides increase from about 6 feet in San Diego and Los Angeles to 10 feet along the Olympic Peninsula in Washington. Ten- to 12-foot ranges are normal from Juneau to Kodiak but decrease westward along the Aleutian Island chain.

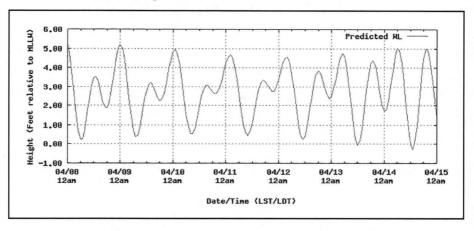

San Diego, CA water level showing Mixed tide over seven days.
5-ft tidal range with different daily patterns.

In the Bering Sea of Alaska, Mixed tides have only 2-foot range and along the North Slope, ranges are even smaller. Tides in Hawaii also are Mixed with 2-foot range. The same for Puerto Rico in the Caribbean—less than 2-foot mixed tides.

• AUTHOR OBSERVATION •

These widely varying geographic variations in tidal characteristics should be in the forefront of captains' minds if they cruise throughout the coastal waters of the U.S., especially in harbors where the entrance channel is prohibitively shallow near low water.

Tidal Currents

Horizontal currents are driven by the vertical movement of water associated with tidal forcing from the moon and sun. In simplest terms, flood tidal currents occur during the incoming, flood tide with strongest flow around midway between the times of high and low water; ebb tidal currents occur similarly during the opposite stage of the tide.

Tidal currents are typically not a major concern in marinas, especially those situated near the heads of harbors where currents are weak or non-existent. If however, a marina is located alongside a major harbor channel or is situated on a riverbank, then tidal flow can impact vessels and marina living in different ways, as listed below and discussed in other sections of this guidebook:

- Docking a vessel can be challenging if tidal currents are perpendicular to the direction of approach, especially for side-tie slips.

- Flushing by tidal currents can be beneficial if wastewater and nuisance algae are swept out of the marina by the horizontal flow.

The best way to prepare for tidal currents in your marina is to become familiar with the times of high and low water, and understand the variations in daily tidal ranges which affect the strength of tidal currents. NOAA websites provide excellent tidal current predictions for numerous locations around the coastal U.S. One of the main NOAA portals for such information is: **http://tidesandcurrents.noaa.gov/currents14**.

CHAPTER 6

Marina Facilities – Important Issues

Safety and Security

GENERAL SAFETY

Basic security awareness is all about knowing your surroundings. If a marina is adjacent to dangerous urban neighborhoods or commercial port facilities, common sense should be the number one deterrent to being victimized. Lighting on your vessel, on the docks, in parking lots and other shore-side facilities (laundry, bathrooms, etc.) also is essential for prevention of theft and vandalism.

It is always best to have your vessel berthed near a few other live-aboard vessels where neighbors can keep an eye on your property during your absence. If you know them reasonably well, inform them of your schedule for departure and return, so that if they notice anyone aboard your vessel they'll know its reason for concern and action.

Thieves by Sea

Shore-side security is foremost on people's mind but boaters must also look in the other direction. Namely, that thieves can and do approach from the water. Theft of an automobile from a parking lot with gated security is much more difficult than coming alongside a vessel in darkness to steal onboard items.

In recent years, many marinas have experienced robbery of floating dinghies and launches tied to their mother vessel or adjacent pier. Owners of small vessels do not need these 'tenders' or 'chase boats' but most vessels above 50 feet in length have dinghies that are convenient for running to shore when the large vessel is anchored out. Normally the dinghies are lifted aboard with a davit or lifting boom then tied down. In this position they are mostly inaccessible by thieves but when large vessels are berthed in a marina or at-anchor in a harbor, the dinghy is often left floating alongside. Some carefree crew tie a couple lines from the dingy to the pier or vessel and all is well — until a thief notices the prospective floating prey. For the thief, it's easy to quietly come alongside in a rowed skiff or kayak, cut two small lines with a knife and tow the dinghy and outboard away. Definitely a small effort to steal a 12-foot rigid inflatable boat, onboard electronics and forty-horsepower, four-stroke outboard, all worth about $30,000. Some larger dinghies and launches have replacement values approaching $100,000.

> **• AUTHOR RECOMMENDATION •**
>
> *Whenever your dinghy is afloat during the night, attach it and its outboard to your vessel with a heavy chain and lock. Keep it well lit and consider a security system or something as simple and inexpensive as a sound monitor like those commonly used in household rooms while babies are sleeping. Waking to voices around your dinghy will give you time and options to deter the thieves.*

There's one more thing to worry about with regard to thieves approaching by water. If your dinghy has a large, expensive outboard, experienced marine thieves can easily unbolt the lower unit of the engine without need for the entire engine to be removed from the dinghy transom. Recently, there have been many lower units stolen from expensive outboards in South Florida, some worth $5,000 each. Five minutes work with a few hand tools and the job is done. If you must leave your motor on the transom of a floating dinghy, lock the motor in the 'down' position because thieves don't like working underwater in the dark.

It's most important to review your vessel insurance policy regarding theft overall and dinghies specifically. Some basic policies exclude dinghies; a rider (add-on policy) must be purchased in such cases. Interestingly, some dinghy policies do not cover the loss of a dinghy if it's being towed, stating that the owner is negligent if the towline is parted. Read the fine print.

Fire Prevention

All vessels must have fire extinguishers onboard that satisfy U.S. Coast Guard requirements, as well as those specified by the vessel insurance policy. However, marinas also are required to have fire prevention equipment on the docks. Most have portable fire extinguishers that can be carried aboard vessels if onboard extinguishers have been fully discharged. Some marinas have fire hoses coiled on vertical stands for use in the event of local fire. Boaters should become familiar with all fire extinguishing systems provided by the marina, whether they are located on the docks or within other buildings of the facility.

When fires occur aboard boats in marinas, neighboring boats are often involved and very quickly. If you are onboard your vessel when fire starts on another vessel in the marina, it is recommended that you immediately move your vessel away from the dock until all fire is extinguished. There is no other way to guarantee that your vessel will not become involved in the fire.

Marina Personnel for Dockside Assistance

Especially for operators of large vessels, having a skilled line handler on the dock while entering or leaving a slip is a tremendous help and added safety for the vessel. Strong winds and currents can pose additional challenges when docking and having someone positioned dockside to tend spring lines is invaluable.

Line-handling assistance can be obtained from boaters of adjacent slips but sometimes they're not around when you need them. In these circumstances it's helpful if the marina can provide a skilled line handler (commonly called a dock boy). At most facilities, docking assistance can be requested from the dockmaster's office either before vessel departure or when entering the marina from sea or elsewhere, via a call using VHF radio.

Of course the 'high-end' marinas with extensive facilities, amenities and support staff have uniformed dock boys available full-time to assist with docking of tenant vessels. This certainly is a valuable service if you own a large vessel.

Boatyard for Haul-Out

Minor boat repairs can normally be conducted while your vessel remains in the water and tied to the dock, as long as the marina tenant agreement permits such maintenance. When major hull work is necessary (e.g., bottom painting or maintenance to through-hull valves, acoustic transducers, engine shafts, cutlass bearings, rudders or propellers), haul-out is typically planned in advance at a boatyard with full capabilities. Without a scheduled haul-out, vessels often have to wait weeks for service.

Emergency haul-out events are rare and normally are necessitated by significant leaks in through-hulls or around keels and running-gear components or caused by collision with rocks, other boats or docks. In such cases, it is ideal if your marina has capabilities to haul vessels of your size. Because yard management personnel know you as a marina tenant, they will usually put you first in line for that day to assure your vessel's safety. Your gratitude will not be overlooked so extend it loudly. It also helps if you contract them to perform additional maintenance work while your vessel is 'on the hard' so they can realize additional revenue.

Compare this situation with one where you have no 'pull' at the only other boatyard in your vicinity. Good luck getting your boat out of the water quickly.

> ## • AUTHOR RECOMMENDATION •
>
> *If you have a chance to become a tenant at a good marina that also has an adjacent, working boatyard, sign up quickly. It's one of the most valuable amenities you will encounter.*

Waste Disposal

NORMAL TRASH

All marinas are responsible for removal of tenant wastes that are placed in well-marked trash containers situated on docks within a short distance of vessels. Recycling bins should be provided by the marina. However, at some poorly managed facilities, tenants are required to carry all trash up the pier to a large shore-based container (e.g., dumpster).  If your slip is located far from the waste container, at least be aware of this when you sign the lease for your slip.

An opposite yet undesirable situation can occur if your slip is located near a large waste container. Odors can be offensive if the container is not emptied often so if a centralized dumpster would be located near your vessel, inquire about the frequency of its emptying. Also note that at some facilities, dumpsters are emptied very early in the morning so you could be dealing with the sound of large waste collection trucks and loud beeping from their back-up sensors.

Become aware of these maintenance functions on your initial visit so they don't surprise you later. If you determine there's only one slip available when you visit a marina, there's a high probability that all existing tenants know that slip has many disadvantages. Some boaters will initially accept the 'bad' slip to get their vessel into the marina but they'll soon request to move when another, more-desirable slip becomes available. Remember that if you're assigned the bad slip and you're not a cooperative tenant, it's likely you'll be berthed there for years.

Oily Wastes

Vessel maintenance can often generate wastes that fall out of the general category of trash. For example, waste oil and engine coolant are typically changed annually and they must be disposed somewhere other than in the container designated for normal trash. The same goes for bilge water that can contain oil and coolant solutions.

Speak with the marina's dockmaster to determine whether the facility has a permanent disposal container for oily wastes. If not, you had better locate a drop-off facility to dispose your oily wastes, presuming your volumes are small and easily transported. On the other hand, if your vessel generates many tens of gallons of oily waste, then it's best to locate a local business (mobile truck or vessel pump-out service) that will come to your vessel for removal of the liquid waste. This topic of oily waste disposal is a very important matter for owners of large vessels. On-site containers provided by the marina are a significant benefit.

Large or Heavy Junk

A simple problem that's easy to understand: most marinas do not allow tenants to place large (i.e., bigger than a suitcase) and/or heavy (i.e., greater than 30 pounds) items of trash in the container designated for normal trash. Boaters are therefore forced to remove these items from the marina facility or pay to have them taken away by a refuse hauling company. Suppliers of large appliances and beds will normally remove the replaced items following delivery of new goods, which fortunately solves the problem for this type of junk. Other more peculiar types of junk are often harder to get rid of. If you believe there is any recycle value (e.g., copper, lead or aluminum) in your junk item, ask the marina's refuse hauling company if they would like to remove it for free.

Be creative and you might not have to pay for junk removal. Most people would be surprised how readily you can sell used marine items on Craigslist.com. For computer savvy folks, post anything you want to get rid of and someone might just call you up and pay to remove your junk.

Channel Access Restrictions

Marinas exist because boaters like to venture out to nearby waters or cruise to distant shores. There are however vessels that always stay tethered to the dock, either as home for live-aboard tenants, for future sale or if the vessel has passed its operational lifetime and the marina hasn't yet evicted 'her'. The majority of vessels that do venture out of the marina expect clear passage within navigable channels but there can be a few challenges, as identified below.

DREDGING INTERFERENCE

Channel deepening operations using mobile, floating dredges are normally accompanied by sediment transport barges and/or large pipes for pumping dredged sediment to nearby beaches or sediment disposal areas. Harbor Masters and U.S. Army Corps of Engineers (ACOE) project managers for the dredging operations normally assure that dredging equipment does not block channel passage but at times this cannot be prevented due to necessary equipment repositioning. The durations of these channel blockages are often short but

there are cases when channels may be blocked for days or longer. If a major dredging project is underway near your marina, contact the on-site ACOE project trailer to inquire about potential channel blockage events if you must transit at a specific time.

EVENTS

A different type of restriction on vessel passage can occur in some large urban harbors during times of boat shows. An example is when a large part of the harbor is consumed by floating docks, thereby restricting vessel movement in close proximity to the show area. A far worse case is when a marina forces all vessels (even long-term tenants) to move out for one to three weeks during a show. Although this might be written into their marina tenant agreement, it might not be mentioned the day you are sign-ing the agreement. It sure can be a big surprise if a boater needs to seek an alternate marina location with only a couple days notice. Similarly, some marinas move their piers to accommodate pedestrian traffic at a show, thus preventing your vessel from leaving her slip for a week or two. Not a good situation if you don't plan ahead.

The dates of major boat shows are known years in advance so consult with the marina office to determine if and how vessel navigation may be adversely affected if a show is planned in your vicinity.

Additional restrictions on vessel passage near your marina can be caused by holiday parades, major sail races, swimming or kayaking events, passage of U.S. Government military vessels, etc.

Handicap Access

All marinas must abide by city ordinances for handicap access but this pri-marily pertains to shore-based facilities (e.g., bathrooms, showers, laundry, etc.). Normally it's the boat owner's responsibility to provide safe and con-venient vessel access for handicapped persons invited aboard. Ramps and steps from the pier to the vessel can generally accommodate this.

The biggest handicap challenge at a marina can be associated with the ramp used for access from shore to the piers. If the marina has a large tidal range, at times of low tide or espe-cially during a Spring tide event, the primary ramps must accommodate a drop of 10 feet or more. This steep-ness is difficult to maneuver even for

people with full capabilities. For those with limited mobility or confinement to a wheel chair, the vertical climb or descent is near impossible. Further, many ramps with handrails are too narrow to accommodate conventional wheel chairs regardless of the ramp's angle from the horizontal.

• AUTHOR RECOMMENDATION •

If you expect to have handicapped persons visit your vessel, be sure to assess the marina's access ramps and gain familiarity with any extreme tidal characteristics of the harbor so that you plan around times of greatest ramp steepness.

Dinghy Storage

This too sounds like a simple topic but sometimes not. Vessels berthed in marinas often keep their dinghies on deck to prevent biofouling of their hull, galvanic corrosion to the outboard motor and theft. At times however, dinghies are used for local fishing, touring the harbor or happy

hour visits at other facilities; consequently they're often kept in the water for a few days. The best situation for temporary, in-water dinghy storage is adjacent to the primary vessel — either tied alongside or off the transom to facilitate easy access and boarding. Many slips provide sufficient space for this type of temporary tie-up but be sure the dockmaster and your tenant agreement permit such practices.

The worst case is a marina that specifies all dinghies must be kept in a designated area, typically some (inconvenient) distance from your vessel. They may even charge a fee for this in-water dinghy storage so beware.

MARINAS

> **· AUTHOR RECOMMENDATION ·**
>
> *Inquire with marina management (or dockmaster); view where other tenants tie their dinghies when in the water; and carefully read the tenant agreement and associated pricing structure.*

Boat Launching Ramp

This guidebook primarily addresses marina use by vessels that are sufficiently large that they're not regularly hauled out of the water on trailers that back into the water via paved ramps. Consequently, having a boat launching ramp at your marina is typically not essential. If however, you wish to haul your dinghy for storage or repair on land, having a nearby ramp for use with a trailer is a major convenience versus having to move your large vessel to a loading dock and lifting with your davit or crane. The dockmaster will know the whereabouts of the nearest launching ramp.

Cable TV Service

Most marinas provide the option for cable TV service on each pier via a coaxial cable connector on the pedestal providing AC power and water to your slip. Typically there is one commercial cable provider so there isn't much to negotiate, except the package you wish to subscribe to, at the quoted price. In some cases, cable TV is included in the price of slip rental.

Some marina cable lines provide, at no charge, local channels from analog TV stations but these have very limited service; typically one channel for local news and ten others with TV shows from the fifties (e.g., Lassie, Andy Griffith, Gilligan's Island, etc.). Seek other options including subscribing to a satellite dish network or installing one of the relatively inexpensive indoor or outdoor digital antennae for capturing local HD TV channels. It is recommended that you consult with a local communications expert to assess options for TV reception on your vessel when berthed at the marina.

Wi-Fi Service

It wasn't many years ago that Wi-Fi was new and established solely for shore-based applications. Fortunately, Wi-Fi service has become another utility that marina owners should provide to boating tenants in order to be competitive. When the technology was new, most marinas would make a half-hearted (low cost) attempt to provide Wi-Fi service to their tenants via a single Wi-Fi antenna mounted on the roof of the marina office. To no surprise, Wi-Fi signal strength, data transmission speed and connectivity were poor except for tenant vessels located very close to the single antenna. Now, most progressive marinas make a greater effort to provide good Wi-Fi service, often installing multiple Wi-Fi antennae at different locations around their facility to guarantee reliability on all piers.

> ### • AUTHOR RECOMMENDATION •
>
> *As you are walking around the marina speaking to any long-term residents, ask them about the Wi-Fi coverage at their pier then ask if they've heard of connectivity problems at other locations in the marina. Just because they might have gotten lucky in their slip doesn't guarantee that other piers have any coverage. If possible, try to determine where any Wi-Fi shadow zones exist before you finalize your slip selection.*

If you need high bandwidth Wi-Fi for business use while aboard your vessel, consider subscribing to an independent commercial Wi-Fi service in the event the marina's free Wi-Fi does not meet your throughput needs.

Postal and Package Delivery

Most marinas that accommodate live-aboard tenants offer mailboxes or at least a delivery point for mail and packages. Some have good mail security (e.g., individual boxes and locked mail facilities after hours) while others handle everything as general delivery and everyone can go through the entire mail pile daily. At these facilities, delivery of important mail or valuable packages is highly discouraged.

Boaters who do not wish to worry about security of their incoming mail should rent a mailbox at the local U.S. Post Office or a private mail/shipping company.

Ship's Store

Most full-service marinas have a Ship's Store for purchase of boating hardware, fishing gear, beverages, take-out food items and minor produce. Some also have fresh and frozen bait for your fishing needs. If you are evaluating two marinas and one has a store open seven days per week, it'll prove to be a major convenience.

Seasonal Considerations

Marinas at mid- and high latitudes normally have seasonal occupancy, with some totally closed and piers removed from the harbor during months of severe storms and likely harbor icing; certainly not the time for a visual marina assessment. At lower latitudes the busy season is during winter when northerners travel south for warm weather and calmer seas than are typical for their homeland. If possible, try to assess marina facilities during maximum occupancy to evaluate tenant congestion, competition for vehicle parking and other marina amenities. Some facilities appear adequate on either side of the 'high season' but parking can be prohibitive during peak occupancy.

CHAPTER 7

Other Marina Considerations

Although it may be surprising to a new boater, there are aspects of marina life, beyond those mentioned above, that you'll encounter and it's always better to learn the tricks early in the game.

Visitors

Boaters enjoy having friends aboard, for offshore excursions and socializing at the dock. Regulations for visitor parking and use of marina facilities vary greatly so be sure to check with the marina office or your tenant agreement to determine what is permissible. For example, some marinas allow boaters' guests to use the pool, exercise room and spa facility while others do not. However, if the guests are staying aboard, then most marinas allow the guests full access to facilities.

Restaurants and Watering Holes

Like anywhere, creature comforts can make life wonderful, even at a marina. When you return from a day of boating it's great to walk a few feet into the marina's restaurant or bar for a quick drink or maybe hours of socializing and dining. Sea stories abound, whether it's good fishing, bad fishing, rough seas, crossing the regatta finishing line first, or nearly sinking because of another marine calamity.

If you have the option of selecting a marina with an on-site or adjacent restaurant versus having none within walking distance, you'll always praise your decision when drowning your sorrows on days when things didn't go perfectly at sea. At some marina restaurants you can take advantage of tenant discounts on drinks and food so inquire about such deals. When marinas don't have a restaurant on-site, marina staff may be able to provide discount coupons for local restaurants and stores.

Launches and Water Taxis

Many marinas are located in areas of prospering waterside businesses and restaurants. Boaters enjoy using their own dinghy or launch for transportation to shopping, dining and Happy Hour visits. However, many dinghies are not lady friendly and nicely dressed women often

prefer taxi transportation rather then face spray and/or rain during the evening's dingy ride.

Upscale marinas and yacht clubs often have one or more reasonably large (i.e., greater than 20-foot) launches for transporting marina tenants and guests short distances to waterfront establishments, moored vessels or other marinas. This service is a fine benefit for individuals

who don't wish to operate small vessels of their own while enjoying an evening's events. A safe and wise decision.

If a marina does not operate its own launch service, some have a nearby (or on-site), privately operated water taxi service available for hire by boaters. This can be very useful but it's essential to determine their operating hours plus their contact phone numbers in the event an emergency arises.

Marina-Provided Ground Transportation

MARINA SHUTTLES

Boat owners certainly run the gamut when it comes to varied lifestyles — some cruising to different marinas with each season while others settle into one location, whether it be for family and employment necessities or for live-aboard retirement. Frequent cruisers normally cannot bring their cars to each location so they must rely on local transportation for shopping, dining, medical and more basic in-town activities. Similarly, some live-aboard retirees shed their vehicles and rely on taxis for all ground transportation.

At some marinas, courtesy vans or shuttle buses are available during normal work hours for tenant transportation to businesses within a few miles of the marina; to airports too. This is a wonderful benefit with considerable cost savings over hired taxis. For after-hours transportation, marinas often have a list of taxis that can be hired, sometimes with a marina discount so be sure to ask.

COURTESY CARS

Many boaters might be pleasantly surprised to hear that some marinas also have a free-use courtesy car that tenants may use for brief, local transportation. A wonderful amenity for sure compared to full-day car rental, often with a considerable cost plus drop-off logistical challenges.

BICYCLES

For active boaters, some marinas maintain a small fleet of bicycles for free tenant use. This is a nice benefit for boaters who are visiting a specific marina for a relatively short period of time and have not brought their own bicycles along for the voyage due to space limitations aboard their vessel.

Marina-provided bicycle racks also can be very useful for temporary storage of owners' bicycles during the period of tenancy. Most marinas provide a sturdy rack at the head of each dock for locking and security. But be sure to remove your bike when departing a marina for the last time so it doesn't add to the unsightly pile of derelict bikes that are seen at some marinas.

Fitness Center and Spa

Many marinas have excellent onshore sporting facilities as attested by their short- and long-term tenants who use them regularly. In contrast, day boaters rarely have time to use the pools, exercise facilities and other sport amenities because they're often busy boating by day or they're back at home by night. Not surprisingly, the best shore-side facilities are typically provided by the more expensive private marinas and yacht clubs but excellent facilities also can be found (and included within reasonable tenant prices) at marinas associated with condominium facilities, hotels and resorts. It's wonderful when marina tenants can enjoy resort-quality living each day they're ashore.

Fitness centers and spas have become one of the most important shore-based amenities that marinas can offer to tenants. Consequently, many boaters make a final choice of a marina based upon the variety and age of the fitness machines, the cleanliness of the exercise facility and spa, and the way it is managed. All of this factors into the overall quality of the exercise experience. Another consideration is the amount of users in the fitness center and spa. Sometimes the best facilities are unusable because of crowding during normal exercise times. If you're an exercise enthusiast, be sure to inspect the marina's fitness center at peak hours before you make a final decision on tenancy.

Swimming Pool and Beaches

Swimming pool facilities also differ greatly among marinas. Some are very attractive, large, well maintained and heated to a constant, comfortable temperature year-round. A few provide purified salt water as an added feature. The poolside amenities also cover a broad range of quality, from large numbers of chairs, tables and chaise lounges at some pools to very modest furniture at others. Unlimited fresh towels are sometimes provided at marina pools associated with large resorts. Surely their management is unaware of this luxury for live-aboard boaters who can 'borrow' a nice supply of towels from the pool area and return them when they are a bit soiled

– a great way for live-aboard boaters to minimize their laundry duties. In summary, don't underestimate the value of a nice pool facility at your marina. Your visiting family members and guests will certainly thank you on each of their visits.

In many desirable locations, marinas have private beaches for use by t.enants and guests. These can be quite modest or exclusive beach facilities with full-time attendants, tiki bars and fine amenities, depending upon the

type of marina. Of course, the best resort facilities offer prime beaches and wonderful amenities. For marinas that don't offer on-site beaches, many provide free shuttle service to nearby public beaches.

Captain's Lounge and Meeting Room

Boaters often like to convene parties at the marina with their friends or family. In some cases, boaters dare mix work with pleasure and convene work-related meetings on site. Small-business owners whose vessel is their primary residence also consider meeting facilities a valuable amenity, especially if they don't have a true place of business. Their clients certainly don't mind meeting in the pleasant environment of an up-scale marina.

Many marinas have wonderful rooms for meetings and parties that can be reserved in advance. This can be a real bonus for the marina tenant depending upon their intended usage. View these facilities during your first on-site visit.

Computer Center

In or adjacent to meeting rooms, some marinas have a computer center for use by tenants. Most offer only tables, chairs and AC power receptacles for tenants to use with their own computers. Other facilities provide a limited number of computers that are available for free usage by marina tenants. All centers now offer free, relatively high-speed access to the marina's Wi-Fi service.

Marinas that are co-located with a resort or hotel facility usually have a business center with full office capabilities and machines for copying, scanning, faxing, etc.

Theater, Game Rooms and Tennis Courts

Yes, some high-end marina facilities (typically those associated with a hotel, apartment complex or condominium facility with many hundreds of tenants) have an on-site theater for free viewing of movies. Quite often, the facility manager will select a different movie to be shown multiple times each day. At some facilities, tenants can play their own movie in the comfort of good seating and with viewing on a big screen. Major televised sporting events also are shown at these private theaters, for the enjoyment of boaters who typically do not have widescreen TVs.

Large facilities sometimes offer rooms with pool tables, video arcades and other gaming devices for adults and children. Some even have squash courts, handball courts and outdoor tennis courts for athletic types. All of these amenities are wonderful additions to marina life, adding to the boaters' resort living.

Rooms and Apartments for Guests

Many full-service marinas have adjacent buildings with rooms and efficiency apartments for rent by marina tenants and their guests. Normally these facilities are limited in numbers and rented on a first-come-first-served basis so inquire early at the marina office to make reservations. In addition to the convenience of having your family or friends staying near your vessel, quite often the daily rate for rental is less than other local hotel or motel facilities.

Mooring Options

Popular marinas often lack capacity to accommodate all of the vessels wishing dockage. Fortunately, some of these marinas have good moorings located nearby where vessels can spend a few nights until slips become available, especially in transient cases. These moorings are typically well maintained, economical and reserved only for boaters planning to enter the marina.

Another advantage of such moorings is that boating friends who wish to visit you but cannot rent a transient slip at your marina due to lack of availability, may spend time on one of the marina's moorings at a good day-rate and within a short dinghy ride to your vessel. This certainly can be a benefit if you're located in a highly popular harbor.

Permissible Maintenance

The amount of maintenance work that can be performed on your vessel while berthed in the slip is a very important factor in marina selection, especially if your vessel is not new. The best-case scenario is when the marina allows owners and their subcontractors to conduct work above and below decks without hassle or oversight. This can save thousands of dollars each year versus having to move the vessel to a boatyard for haul-out and repair. If you encounter this good situation, be careful not to abuse this privilege. Read the fine-print of the marina tenant agreement for any guidelines but most importantly, consider the following:

1. Speak with other boaters who have worked on their vessel to determine what they think is permissible

2. Understand that you cannot allow significant amounts of particulate matter (i.e., paint chips) to enter the water because that will violate water quality regulations

3. Don't let airborne particulates blow onto adjacent piers or vessels, and

4. Keep the noise down so it doesn't bother your neighbors. Follow these recommendations and you'll be able to work moderately and save yourself lots of money.

The only potential downside of marinas allowing work aboard vessels is that you might have to contend with noise from work on adjacent vessels and hopefully not particulates blowing aboard your boat when the wind is right.

Most importantly, you don't want to be situated in a floating boatyard or equivalent maintenance facility with workers beginning at 7 a.m. and finishing after dark, even on weekends. This can be a bad experience so look around the marina during your first visit to determine the level of maintenance being conducted on vessels.

Fishing from Docks and Vessels

Marina guidelines typically specify whether fishing is permitted from docks and berthed vessels. Although fishing is often disallowed, most facilities don't uphold this policy, especially if tenants don't create high visibility and/or leave bait or fish remains on the piers as they attract sea birds and possibly rodents.

In some harbors, large schools of baitfish congregate and allow for easy catches with lines or cast nets. This is a major benefit for fishermen who know the best procedures for catching these species. A major cost savings too, versus having to buy bait from local retailers.

Although edible species can sometimes be caught at your marina, do not eat any fish or crustaceans caught locally. They likely have ingested cleaning products, bilge water or possibly human and toxic wastes discharged from vessels. Especially be sure not to eat crabs or lobsters that feed on bottom species and undesirable material that sinks from the surface. Also, never eat whole, uncooked clams, oysters or mussels because they siphon large volumes of water and accumulate chemicals, unhealthy particulates and contaminated bacteria within their stomachs. Scallops are the exception because only the shell's hinge muscle is eaten; not the stomach.

Except for bait fishing, catch-and-release is the only advisable fishing technique within marinas and harbors. It's for your safety, not an overzealous marina restriction.

Availability of Dock Carts

Seasoned live-aboard boaters know the importance of dock carts. They're essential for transporting engine parts, groceries, heavy cases of beverages and other purchases down the dock. If your vessel is located 100 yards or more from the parking lot, this transport task certainly can be a major challenge and the  cart is your savior. Some marinas provide dozens of well-designed carts for tenant use whereas other marina situations are less than optimal with regard to cart quality and availability. In such cases, a few carts must be shared by hundreds of vessels and sometimes they contain wet paint, oil or other wastes from vessel maintenance. Often it's necessary to have your own cart and keep it onboard to prevent theft. At good marinas, this issue is a non-problem because management is doing their job with regard to facility resources and management.

Storage Boxes on the Docks

Tenants are not permitted to place boating paraphernalia on the pier adjacent to their vessel. Relatively large, white dock boxes are typically allowed on the pier, in addition to a small volume of  other items such as hoses and fenders, as long as they do not clutter the dock and become a hazard to passersby.

Although some marinas have detailed specifications on what type of dock boxes are permitted at their facility, most are flexible about dockside storage and allow bicycles and other tenant belongings to be kept on the dock adjacent to their vessel. Such flexibility is good for the tenant who owns lots of 'stuff' but some, hopefully not your boating neighbor, can abuse this privilege.

• AUTHOR RECOMMENDATION •

Walk the docks and view your potential neighborhood to see if your adjacent tenants have significant clutter that is likely to sprawl into your space or dock access area. If so, verify that marina management will address this problem rather than having you be the individual to confront Mr. Sloppy. Such discussions with obstinate boaters often lead to irreversible rifts.

Vending Machines

Many boaters believe that coin-operated vending machines for purchase of snacks, bottled water and soft drinks are an important amenity for marinas. The quality of products sold and the frequency of restocking are certainly essential for customer satisfaction.

Water Toys

During the past couple decades there has been a tremendous increase in development and use of personal water craft. Nowadays many boaters also are avid users of paddleboards, sailboards, small sailing craft, kayaks, jet skis and other water toys.

Most own their toys and keep them on their berthed vessels. Other boaters (and their guests) don't own such toys but given the opportunity, they surely would rent the item of their choice from the marina for an hour or two. Similarly, some facilities have scuba equipment to rent to tenants. For this reason, many active boaters appreciate that their marina (or resort) has a fleet of water toys for easy rental. In some cases, the marina allows a separate small business to lease some of their dockage for rental of toys, in collaboration with marina guidelines and security restrictions, of course.

Community Garden

Many live-aboard boaters establish permanent residency aboard their vessel regardless of its size. In such cases, they're often challenged by not having their own garage, attic, basement or back yard for storage of boating paraphernalia or cherished possessions. Similarly, they don't have a plot of land for planting their favorite flowers or vegetables. To the good fortune of live-aboard folks, some family-friendly marinas offer garden plots for use by long-term tenants. This is much appreciated by users and certainly worth inquiring about if you're seeking a marina for long-term residency.

Birds and Sea Life

Marinas provide a wonderful vantage point for observing various types of sea life and coastal birds. Of course, everyone loves to view diverse species in their natural habitat but there are situations when mingling with nature don't work out so well.

BIRDS

Great blue herons are majestic, gray shore birds that stand 3 feet tall on stilt-like legs and have four-inch-long bills for snatching fish from shallow waters beneath their penetrating stare. Their necks can extend 2 feet to catch fish or raise their heads with curiosity. Mostly solitary, they sometimes land on a pier and scan downward for their next meal. If they visit a specific pier often, their natural painting becomes quite notice-able and odoriferous.

Normally herons maintain a safe, cautious distance from humans but one such character (gender unknown) befriended me while my vessel was berthed in a San Diego marina. "Harriet" would actually land on the cock-pit gunnel to see if I had any fresh bait to share. On one occasion when I was working down in the lazarette (storage hold) beneath the cockpit, my wife whispered for me to look up. There was Harriett standing on the deck at the edge of the opening peering down to see what I was doing. A surpris-ing action from such a solitary species. Unfortunately, Harriett's dock paint was no less voluminous or scented than that of her fellow herons.

Smaller shore birds also can become regular visitors aboard vessels, partly from curiosity and gradual lack of fear. This is enjoyable from the bird-watcher's perspective but cleaning duties accompany the rewards. Cormorants have the most caustic excrement but fortunately, they prefer to keep a safe distance from humans and active docks.

Gulls are the worst winged visitors and they deserve the moniker flying rats. These culprits can be very aggressive, sometimes swooping down toward a boater and snatching food from their hand or plate. If food is left outdoors and unattended when gulls are around, count on it being stolen within seconds.

· AUTHOR RECOMMENDATION ·

Don't toss food or bait to gulls or you'll soon be inundated by a large, pesky flock that won't disperse.

At some marina locations, small black birds congregate in large numbers on nearby trees and remain in the vicinity for periods of days to weeks. Oftentimes they venture onto adjacent boats, perched in the rigging of sailboats or on the superstructure of tall powerboats. This definitely becomes a problem with bird droppings and boaters mount fake owls and/or install whirligigs of various designs as attempts to keep the birds away, often to no avail.

MAMMALS

Seals and sea lions also are wonderful to view in their natural environs, swimming by and feeding on schools of anchovies, herring and other species. However, they too can become a nuisance, especially when they leap aboard swim platforms of vessels, as is the case in many West Coast harbors and marinas. Once aboard, they are difficult to move by mild encouragement yet environmentalists and some regulatory agencies scorn more forceful techniques.

• AUTHOR RECOMMENDATION •

If seals are prevalent in your harbor, construct a barrier to obstruct their access to your swim platform, cockpit or dinghy. Don't allow them to make the first move, block them, in a harmless way of course.

Nuisance Algae

Certain types of marine algae can be a sight, odor and/or toxicity problem for boaters and swimmers. Examples of three types are discussed below, although there are likely more.

RED TIDE

Harmful algal blooms are often called Red Tides although they have nothing to do with tides. Such blooms (high concentrations of floating aquatic plants) can be caused by a sudden and temporary excess of nutrients added to the water of a coastal area, harbor or brackish coastal pond by either of three processes:

1. Nutrient discharge from human activities

2. Natural upwelling of nutrient-rich waters from an adjacent, deeper source, or

3. Wind-born iron- or nutrient rich sediments blown into coastal waters

Natural toxins in shellfish can be generated by Red Tides and they can be fatal if eaten raw. Additionally, the explosion of algal growth subsequently depletes the dissolved oxygen of the water, causing the local marine system to become anoxic (absent of oxygen) and the flora and fauna living in the immediate vicinity die off quite rapidly. The decaying organic matter gives off offensive odors.

In some coastal areas of New England (especially Rhode Island), a natural type of red seaweed (much larger than the microscopic phytoplankton associated with Red Tide) can accumulate in coves and harbors from the action of prevailing winds. This type of weed grows on rocky seafloor;

fastest during warm, late-summer months. Heavy surf can rip the mature plants from the bottom but they continue to grow as a free-floating plant. This type of weed is neither harmful nor toxic but can become a major nuisance when accumulated in large masses. When rain and contaminated runoff are absorbed by the seaweed, offensive odors can develop in association with human and/or animal fecal bacteria trapped in the weed mass. The weed is blamed but the odors are associated with the land-based contributions. Typically the weed and odor will remain until fall storms and surge carry the weed out to sea.

In the shallow, warm waters along the southwest coast of Florida, aquatic weeds and organic matter grow rapidly, settle to the seafloor and are consumed by natural bacteria. Surprisingly, much of this bacterial decomposition occurs in the bottom sediment rather than in the water or on the seabed. Because the overlying waters become oxygen depleted, a special type of bacteria begins to thrive and generate hydrogen sulfide gas that smells like rotten eggs (FBAMS, 2000). In many areas, the strong, offensive smell is a common occurrence in the shallow-water ecosystem, giving adjacent beaches and marinas a horrible smell that lingers for months. The water may also contain toxic chemicals that are dangerous on contact or if ingested, so swimmers must beware.

• AUTHOR RECOMMENDATION •

If algal problems are known to occur in the vicinity of your preferred marina, investigate these potential problems carefully because such odors can make your marina life horrible. Speak to locals and search online for newspaper articles on local algal problems during warm months. If you happen to visit a marina when it's offseason for the specific algal problem, you could be very disappointed the next warm season when your nose encounters the odors.

Unwanted Pests

Shorelines of harbors and marinas can sustain healthy populations of rodents, reptiles and insects. Additionally, some species flourish beneath docks that foster marine growth and constant moisture. If major infestations occur, it is the responsibility of marina management to have professional exterminators come on-site to rid the area of unwanted pests. Tenants should inform marina management if pests become prevalent.

Boat owners should take precautions to prevent pests from coming aboard. If rodents and reptiles exist at the marina, it is recommended that gangways to vessels be removed at night to deter walk-ons. If this is not possible or convenient, repellent sprays and powders can be applied to the bottom (shore-side end) of the ramp and around the base.

Smaller pests and insects frequently come aboard via dock lines, power cords and hoses. Application of repellents may be necessary on these routes also.

Don't overlook the most common route for insects to come aboard — via your carry-on produce. Also, if you have on-shore storage, either a dock box or a large storage unit off-site, it is possible that your stored items contain pests and they will come aboard with your assistance. If you have concern, it's best to unpack all items on the pier or on-deck to be sure none are waiting to be carried below to your living areas.

Regardless of these precautions, insects do come aboard. As soon as any are visible, use appropriate repellents to exterminate them and leave residual chemicals to rid unseen others. If they persist, it is strongly recommended that a professional exterminator be hired for spraying in all below-deck areas. Marina personnel likely know of good local professionals. Note that to rid persistent insects and roaches, it is necessary that the boat be sprayed at 2-week intervals for at least three cycles to ensure that all pests are gone. The cost of each spraying event will depend upon vessel size but for a 50-footer, it may be $30 to $50. Compare this to the cost of a motel room if you're driven off the boat from pest infestations and you'll realize it's a wise investment.

No matter how diligent you are about pest control, odd occurrences do arise. One sunny day in Florida I returned to my vessel in the afternoon. Hearing a noise on the flying bridge, I went up to determine the source. There, sitting on the helm beneath the wind block was a 3-foot long, iridescent iguana. Beautiful he was, but not welcome aboard my boat. Using a long-handled scrub brush, he was escorted down the stairs and into a tote bag for a quick lift to the wooded area of the parking lot, hopefully never to be seen aboard again. My first guess was that a friend had pulled a practical joke on me by tossing the iguana aboard but local residents said it happens once in a while at these low latitudes. It sure would have been a big surprise if he had walked across my bed during the night.

Airborne Dirt

The frequency of boat washing (and costs for hired services, if necessary) is largely dependent upon the amount of airborne dirt at your marina. Don't overlook this dirt issue when you're viewing potential marinas for your vessel. Potential sources are listed below:

- Unpaved, dirt parking lots at or adjacent to the marina

- Major highways within a half mile of the marina

- Large, overhead bridges for autos or railroads
- Airports within a couple miles with frequent flights of large jets

First-hand experience has proven that if any of the above conditions are met at your marina, you'll have to wash your boat at least once per week or each time you visit your vessel if you don't live aboard. Sounds like a minor inconvenience but if you're in one of these 'dirty' marinas and you plan to leave your boat unattended for a month or longer, you'll face quite a mess when you return if a boat cleaning service had not been enlisted during your absence. Accept this inevitability when you sign your tenant agreement and don't bitch about it later.

Offensive Odors

Marinas usually take care to keep major waste containers away from the piers but boaters can be impacted by other nearby sources of offensive odors. Watch out for these offensive smelling neighbors when you are assessing a marina:

- Stagnant bays, salt marshes and ponds that are prone to harmful algal blooms
- Fleets of commercial fishing vessels
- Sewage treatment plants within a couple miles of the marina
- Waste disposal or recycling facilities
- Commercial fish processing plants

The wind direction on the day of your visit to a marina may be favorable, but ask existing tenants whether any of these odors become a problem when the winds change direction.

Sources of Noise

Marina tenant agreements normally specify how boaters should minimize noise, such as running their engines at the dock only for short periods of time (say 15 minutes or less) before departure or during periods of engine maintenance. Similarly, boaters are warned that noise from barking dogs, playing musical instruments and onboard parties should be held to a reasonable level and curtailed altogether after 10 p.m.

Sources of noise also can pose problems to peaceful boating life in the marina such as:

- Commercial fishing boats which sometimes depart before sunrise

- Clanging halyard lines on neighboring sailboats that can be remedied by rubber cords

- Nearby construction projects using noisy pile-drivers and cranes, such as at adjacent marinas or bridge construction sites

- Adjacent highways, bridges, railways and airports

It is always wise to drive around a marina, look for signs of major construction projects and transportation pathways, and speak with existing marina tenants to learn about major sources of noise that could adversely affect the quality of your marina stay.

· CHAPTER 8 ·
Vessel Considerations and Services

Galvanic Corrosion and Stray Current

GALVANIC CORROSION

All vessels are victim to galvanic corrosion (often called marine electrolysis), which is initiated by dissimilar metals that are in electrical contact with each other while immersed in seawater, an effective electrolytic solution. Galvanic corrosion also can be initiated from other nearby vessels, from large metal objects on the harbor bottom or from any metal pilings of the seawall at the head of the dock, if close to the vessel (say within 50 feet). Note that freshwater is a poor conductor of electricity therefore vessel corrosion from neighboring sources is much less of a concern than in saltwater. When seawater is warm, corrosion is accelerated as in Florida compared to New England.

To retard corrosion, zincs (sacrificial anodes) are attached to the vessel's submerged metal components of exposed running gear and through-hull fittings. Additionally, heavy-gauge, green plastic-jacketed wire is attached to all metal components within the boat that have through-hull contact with the seawater. It is essential that the entire 'bonding system' has electrical continuity and is well maintained; otherwise, individual metal components will be 'floating' (i.e., electrically independent of the zinc anodes) and excessive, local corrosion will result from leaking current.

The rate of corrosion can be increased when a vessel connects to shore power unless the vessel is well bonded or isolated by a special type of marine-certified isolation transformer. Corrosion effects are typically worse at small marinas where the vessel is situated close to submerged metal shore structures (i.e., retaining walls) versus piers of large marinas that are considerably farther from metal shore structures.

STRAY CURRENT

If a marina is considered hot from an electrical standpoint, there are two possible sources: 1) the shore power cable is carrying stray current, or 2) the seawater is carrying stray current, possibly from an adjacent vessel. If you believe there is excessive stray current being released from an adjacent boat or any electrical equipment mounted on the pier, a simple source-identification test can be conducted at various locations around the dock using a basic voltmeter.

It is important to understand the differences between a safety issue for the vessel versus safety issues for humans. For example, galvanic corrosion (weak DC release) can slowly dissolve a propeller whereas stray AC current in the water can electrocute a swimmer. Keep in mind the difference between bonding for galvanic corrosion, stray current in the boat, stray current outside the boat and galvanic corrosion surrounding the boat. Causes of galvanic corrosion were discussed above.

Stray current in a vessel is common and easily tested by a marine electrician. A stray wire in the bilge originating from a submerged bilge pump causes one example. Stray current from outside a vessel is DC; AC does not cause stray current corrosion. On some facilities, DC current is dangerously carried through the AC ground (the green wire) to and from shore. Adding a galvanic isolator is a substantial expense but it would eliminate this type of stray current problem.

> ### • AUTHOR RECOMMENDATION •
>
> *If any problem is encountered with your shore power, contact an electrical technician, either from the marina or from a local, fully insured service company. Remember: Never disconnect the green ground wire from the shore power cable. This could put all persons aboard your vessel at risk of electrical shock or death.*

Biofouling – The Light Stuff

Vessels that are routinely berthed in marinas encounter biological growth on their submerged hulls. The majority of this growth is associated with local aquatic species but non-indigenous marine species also can make up part of the biological community, attaching themselves when the vessel visited other ports. In basic terms, biofouling is an accumulation of micro-organisms, algae, marine plants and animals.

PROBLEMS CREATED BY BIOFOULING

When fouling becomes significant, it has adverse effects on the hydrodynamics of the vessel, with increased drag and associated speed reduction for an underway vessel. It is not uncommon for a 'fouled' vessel to experience 10 percent loss of speed. If engine RPMs are increased to achieve normal speed, fuel consumption may increase by 20 to 40 percent.

In addition to hull fouling, biological growth on engine shafts, bearings and propellers can cause excess strain on the drive train of the propulsion system and loss of propeller efficiency. Fouling-induced friction and reduced mobility in rudder components can add significant stress to steering mechanisms and cause malfunction. These effects must be prevented by anti-fouling methods and postponement will only make the problem worse.

THE BIOLOGICAL PROCESS OF FOULING

The first stage of fouling on a clean hull occurs during the first week it is immersed. Initially, a biofilm is developed from bacteria that adhere to the surface. This stage, called microfouling, does not significantly increase hull drag but it does create a surface upon which macrofouling can begin. During the second and third weeks, a wide variety of marine organisms eagerly attach to the film. Hard fouling organisms include barnacles, mollusks (including zebra mussels and others) and tube worms which have rigid casings. Soft fouling organisms also flourish on the surface, with growth of seaweed, algae and soft animals such as hydroids and slime. Within one month, an active biological community develops — ideal for analysis by the marine biologist but a significant problem for the boater.

Note that availability of a host surface is necessary for macrofouling. As soon as the hard organisms are able to settle in, they become an ideal surface for others to adhere to. This results in a rapid increase in population density and addition of more soft fouling organisms.

PREVALENCE OF BIOFOULING

Marine biologists around the globe have conducted many studies of the incidence of biofouling on recreational vessels. Some of the key findings are given below:

- Warm waters accelerate biofouling.

- Berthing a vessel adjacent to piers, pilings or other structures with established biological communities fosters propagation of organisms to the vessel.

- Vessels with prolonged inactivity yield more biofouling development than an active vessel that is underway frequently.

- Vessels moored in a harbor tend to have more biofouling than vessels berthed at piers, primarily a result of moored vessels being used less frequently and having their hulls maintained seldom.

- Underway vessels prohibit initiation of marine growth and expel some of the established biofouling communities via the forces of water and waves which apply horizontal friction to the hull.

- Vessels that travel at high speeds shed biofouling organisms more effectively than slower vessels.

- Loss of speed and costs of wasted fuel from biofouling hull drag are strong incentives for owners to apply anti-fouling coatings to their vessel.

Brief History of Anti-Fouling Methodology

As far back as 1,500 B.C., mariners encountered biofouling and sought to alleviate the problem with hull applications of pitch, tar and wax. Around 400 B.C. the effectiveness of toxic chemicals for retarding biological growth was discovered and mixtures of oil, sulfur and arsenic were used to coat hulls as a deterrent for wood-boring shipworms.

In the 1700s, copper plating was applied over wood hulls with good anti-fouling success but with new construction of iron-hull vessels in the 1800s, copper plating became a major problem as it induced galvanic corrosion from the bonded dissimilar metals.

Not until the 1960s was there a major breakthrough for anti-fouling coatings, with development of organo-tin chemicals (i.e., tributyl-tin: TBT). As an anti-fouling coating is hydrolized in seawater, it slowly releases chemicals that are toxic to marine organisms. Hulls coated with TBT paints were mostly growth-free for periods up to 4 years in some regions. This was a major benefit for biofouling of recreational, commercial and naval vessels but TBT was later discovered to be highly toxic to mollusks and other marine organisms whose tissue could pass through the food chain to humans. Consequently, in the 1980s TBT was banned on vessels less than 25 meters in length. The use of organotin compounds as biocides in anti-fouling paint was completely banned in 2008 by the International Maritime Organization.

Present Day Types of Anti-Fouling

Biocides and non-toxic coatings are the two most widely used categories of anti-fouling chemicals in practice today. Biocides are added to anti-fouling surface coatings to attack film-producing aquatic bacteria. These copper-based (cuprous oxide) anti-fouling solutions are much less toxic than the earlier organotins but are generally effective with fewer adverse impacts on the marine environment.

Non-toxic coatings, primarily organic polymers, create a very smooth surface and thereby prevent attachment of marine organisms to the coated hulls. These fluoropolymers and silicone coatings are ecologically inert which is a major advantage over the organotins. However, they are still in early stages of perfection and have disadvantages of limited mechanical strength and long-term stability.

Hydrophilic coatings also are being developed for anti-fouling applications but they and other methods are still in Research and Development stages, and thus prohibitively expensive for recreational boaters.

Because the technology for anti-fouling coatings is advancing rapidly, boat owners should consult with major distributors of marine paints to determine best products and the associated terminology. Hard-coat paints are typically used on fast boats (i.e., greater than 20 knot speeds) because they are less prone to washing off by friction on the hull. Ablative (soft-coat) paints purposely shed their coating slowly but quicker under the action of water friction so they are not recommended on fast boats. Vessel characteristics, frequency of hauling and bottom cleaning, water temperature, local rates of fouling and other factors must be considered when selecting the best anti-fouling paint for your vessel.

Invasive Non-indigenous Mussels — The Worst Biofouling

Rapid reproduction and geographic spread of non-indigenous aquatic organisms is a major problem in fresh and saline environments of the U.S. In recent years, invasive lionfish have received broad public attention because of their decimation of reef fish in tropical waters (and their natural photographic appeal). They certainly are a major problem for co-located fisheries but infestations of nuisance mussels presently have far greater negative impact on native species and human health in the U.S. Additionally, they cause negative impacts to vessels, economically important fish and shellfish, and industrial facilities that rely on flow of natural waters for cooling.

This section provides an overview of major mussel species to familiarize the reader with the biological characteristics and potential impacts of each within U.S. waters. The majority of information provided herein came from Wikipedia.com, which proved to be a good source for general information on mussel species. Other more-specific, scientific articles on individual mussel species are given on that website.

Zebra Mussels	
Species:	Dreissena Polymorpha (Dreissena is the name of an extinct zebra species)
Native region:	Rivers and lakes of Eastern Europe and western Asia
History in U.S.A.:	• Entered U.S.A. in ballast water of trans-oceanic ships. • First discovered in U.S.A. in the Great Lakes in 1988

Zebra Mussels	
Geographic range in U.S.A:	• Throughout Great Lakes and down Mississippi River. • Also present in states south of Great Lakes • Atlantic coast is clear, from Florida to New York
Problem level:	Severe
Known predators in U.S.A.:	None
Preferred environment:	Attachment to hard surfaces and flow intake pipes
Adverse impacts:	• Depletion of dissolved oxygen in water • Suffocation of local shellfish by attachment. Densities up to 35,000 mussels per square meter • Clogging of water intake pipes and submerged pumps • Encrustation of vessels, buoys and coastal structures
Positive impacts:	Water clarity is improved by filtering of particulates
Shell size:	1 to 2 inches
Preferred aquatic environment:	• Freshwater only • Can withstand cold temperatures
Reproduction cycle:	• Growth, over-wintering and reproduction • Strong filter feeders (1 liter of water per day)
Mussel's food source:	Algae (phytoplankton)

Zebra Mussels	
Saltwater relative:	Dark false mussel (native to Atlantic Coast)
Food appeal in U.S.A.:	• None – contaminated shellfish • Major accumulators of toxic chemicals in mussel tissue

Quagga Mussels	

Species:	Dreissena Bugenis
Native region:	Ukraine in western Asia
History in U.S.A.:	• Entered U.S. in ballast water via St. Lawrence seaway • First discovered in U.S.A. in the Great Lakes in 1989
Geographic range in U.S.A:	• Throughout Great Lakes • In 2008, spread to Colorado River, southern California, western Arizona and Southern Nevada • Atlantic coast and Gulf of Mexico are quagga free
Problem level:	Severe
Known predators in U.S.A.:	None
Preferred environment:	Attachment to hard surfaces and flow intake pipes

Quagga Mussels	
Adverse impacts:	• Depletion of dissolved oxygen in water • Suffocation of local shellfish by attachment. Densities up to 35,000 mussels per square meter • Clogging of water intake pipes and submerged pumps • Encrustation of vessels, buoys and coastal structures
Positive impacts:	Water clarity is improved by filtering of particulates
Shell size:	Small (coin sized)
Preferred aquatic environment:	• Freshwater only • Can withstand cold temperatures
Reproduction cycle:	• Strong filter feeders (1 liter of water per day). • Prolific breeders: 1 million eggs per year
Mussel's food source:	Algae (phytoplankton)
Food appeal in U.S.A.:	• None – contaminated shellfish • Major accumulators of toxic chemicals in mussel tissue. (300,000 times greater than concentrations in natural environment)

ATTEMPTS TO ESTABLISH AQUATIC PREDATORS FOR QUAGGA MUSSELS

In 2004, it was determined that yellow perch would feed on quagga mussels but in doing so they would ingest toxic chemicals that had been accumulated in high concentrations by the mussels. This could lead to another, possibly larger problem if perch tissue were ingested by mammals, birds and humans, thus bringing the contaminants higher into the natural food chain. Similarly, redear sunfish were later discovered to prey naturally on quagga mussels and they have been introduced in the Colorado River system despite the potential of establishing routes for food-chain transfer.

Asian Green Mussels	
65 mm	
Species:	Perna Viridis
Native region:	• Indo-Pacific region • An economically important shellfish species in Asia due to its food quality when raised in clean aquaculture facilities.
History in U.S.A.:	• Entered Caribbean region via ballast water in 1990 • First discovered in U.S.A. in Tampa Bay in 1999 • Most recent non-indigenous mollusk to invade Florida
Geographic range in U.S.A:	• Southern coasts of Florida • Atlantic coast to South Carolina (southern temperate areas) • Spread along Atlantic coast is likely due to larval drift by currents
Problem level:	Severe
Known predators in U.S.A.:	None
Preferred environment:	Attachment to hard surfaces and flow intake pipes

Asian Green Mussels	
Adverse impacts:	• Depletion of dissolved oxygen in water • Suffocation of local shellfish by attachment. Densities up to 35,000 mussels per square meter • Clogging of water intake pipes and submerged pumps • Encrustation of vessels, buoys and coastal structures
Positive impacts:	Water clarity is improved by filtering of particulates
Shell size:	Can grow to 3 to 4 inches in length
Preferred aquatic environment:	• Wide range of acceptable marine conditions. • Prefers regions of high water flow. • Saltwater and brackish environments (18 to 33 ppt) • Temperatures ranging from 50° to 90° F
Reproduction cycle:	• Strong filter feeders (1 liter of water per day).
Mussel's food source:	Algae (phytoplankton)
Food appeal in U.S.A.:	• None – contaminated shellfish • Major accumulators of toxic chemicals in mussel tissue. • Deadly if accumulating dinoflagellate phytoplankton from seawater

Asian Green Mussels are relatively new to U.S. coastal waters but have already become a major biofouling problem for vessels berthed in wet slips in Florida and the southeast U.S. coastline. Mussel fouling of industrial facilities also is highly problematic for those having seawater intake pipes and pumps.

Brown Mussels	
Species:	Perna Perna
Native region:	• West Coast of Africa and coast of South America to Caribbean • Excellent food appeal in South America and Africa
History in U.S.A.:	First aquatic invasion was in Texas; accidental via ballast water from Venezuela
Shell size:	Typically 2.5 to 4 inches in length
Color:	Brown
Preferred aquatic environment:	Can exist in a broad range of salinity and temperature
Biofouling potential:	High but can be controlled by chlorination

ADDRESSING THE PROBLEM OF MUSSEL INFESTATION ON VESSELS

Returning to the principal topic of this book, boaters are faced with two problems from invasive mussels:

1. Biofouling of vessel hulls which causes speed reduction and fuel waste, and

2. Infestation of mussels within through-hull fittings and 'raw water' lines to pumps (e.g., for air conditioning pumps for coolant water

flow, for toilets using saltwater for flushing, for saltwater wash-down pumps and for inflow to live-bait wells).

Additionally, raw water is pumped in high volume to engines and generators for cooling. It is critical for efficient vessel operations that all of these intake lines be free of obstructions.

If a vessel's raw water lines become infested with nuisance mussels inboard of the through-hull fittings (and thus inaccessible by diver cleaning) either the lines must be replaced or cleaned by an intensive flow-through process using a commercially available product such as Barnacle Buster. This liquid cleaner is a non-toxic (to humans) biodegradable solution designed to remove marine growth from interior surfaces of hoses, pipes and valves. The solvent is added to a large volume of clean freshwater and pumped through the lines to a recirculating reservoir and filtering system to remove mussels, barnacles and other unwanted deposits. Thorough cleaning can typically be accomplished after two to four hours of circulating solution.

METHODS TO PREVENT FURTHER SPREAD OF INVASIVE MUSSELS

For boaters who operate in regions with non-indigenous invasive species, it is important they take actions to prevent further spreading of these unwanted species to other geographic regions. Recommended procedures (Best Practices) are given below:

- Be aware of invasive species that exist in your local waters.

- For vessels kept in wet slips, conduct periodic bottom cleaning to thoroughly remove all mussels attached to the hull, running gear and through-hull fittings.

- If possible, conduct bottom cleaning while the vessel is on land to prevent the scrapings from reentering the water.

- Immediately before cruising to another area, ensure that no mussels or non-native fouling organisms are attached to your vessel.

- Empty bilges and live-well bait tanks of water before cruising and be sure to dispose of the water on land or in proper liquid-waste containers.

Non-Invasive Mussel Species

It is relatively easy to confuse the various mussel species, especially recognizing that in the U.S., green mussels of Asian descent are generally poisonous if harvested in U.S. waters but green mussels imported from New Zealand are an excellent food source and consequently, are widely available in the U.S. To help the average consumer and concerned boater, basic characteristics are given below for mussels not categorized as invasive in the U.S. although most are non-indigenous.

New Zealand Green-Tipped Mussel

Species:	Perna Canalicula
Native region:	• New Zealand only • Great importance as a cultivated species
History in U.S.A.:	Strictly imported for human consumption
Shell size:	Up to 9 inches in length; largest species of mussel
Color:	Dark brown/green shell except for green-tips around edge
Temperature environment:	Cannot live in tropics
Food appeal in U.S.A.:	Excellent imported species
Possible medicinal value:	• Some believe this mussel has natural healing characteristics, including anti-inflammation and pain relief. • Marketed for treating arthritis and joint problems.

European (Mediterranean) Blue Mussels

Species:	Mytilus Galloprovincialis
Native region:	• Mediterranean and Black Seas • Suitable for aquaculture
History in U.S.A.:	Introduced to West Coast around 1900
Shell size:	3 to 5 inches in length
Color:	Blue
Temperature environment:	Cold waters
Food appeal in U.S.A.:	Excellent

California Mussels

Species:	Mytilus Californianus
Native region:	• West Coast of North America • Strong natural species; not cultivated
Shell size:	3 to 5 inches in length but up to 9 inches

California Mussels	
Color:	Blue
Temperature environment:	High salinity, preferably clear water, rough conditions
Food appeal in U.S.A.:	Excellent

Blue (Common) Mussels	
Species:	Mytilus Edulis
Native region:	• Both Coasts of North Atlantic and North Pacific • Also in southern Hemisphere
Shell size:	3 to 5 inches in length
Color:	Blue
Temperature environment:	• Temperate to polar waters • Intensive aquaculture
Food appeal in U.S.A.:	Excellent

Bottom Cleaning

The following discussion pertains to relatively large vessels that are kept afloat for the boating season (at higher latitudes) or throughout the year in southern waters. Bottoms of small boats that are not marina residents can easily be washed each time they come out of the water and trailered. Larger vessels can either be scrubbed while berthed in the marina or when hauled out of the water for repairs or inspection. Regardless of vessel size, each hull should be power-washed and scraped to remove marine fouling organisms. During this process, it is essential that the organic debris and rinse water be collected and disposed according to local regulations for wastewater.

This task sounds very simple but don't fool yourself into thinking there aren't subtleties a boat owner needs to be aware of. Read the list below for starters.

- Bottom cleaners must be cognizant of local regulations that specify the types of tools and procedures to be used at their location. New regulations arise each year on account of growing concern about pollution of the marine environment, with some states such as California being very aggressive on restrictions for bottom cleaning. Beware.

- Ask your bottom cleaner if he/she is knowledgeable of non-indigenous mussel species and how to recognize them.

- Not all bottom cleaners know what they're doing. Ask marina management if they recommend any local, reputable individuals or bottom cleaning companies.

- Disreputable bottom cleaners may clean only around the water line of a vessel as it's the only part of the hull that can be seen by the owner standing on the pier. This actually occurs.

- Many trustworthy bottom-cleaning companies now offer underwater videography services to show the boat owner the condition of the hull before and after cleaning. This is an excellent capability as it also demonstrates the effectiveness of the cleaning process. It is wise to hire a company that offers this type of video service, at no extra charge.

- Professional bottom cleaning companies often encourage boat owners to subscribe to a regular schedule (i.e., monthly) for cleaning. The frequency of this service should be questioned by the boat owner to ensure it is necessary and not too often for their seawater environment and boat usage regimen. Ask owners of neighboring boats what is their best bottom-cleaning schedule.

- Frequent cleanings are recommended but they each erode some of the anti-fouling coating, especially the ablative materials and/or if the cleaning tools are inappropriately rough. The cleanest hulls may require more frequent anti-fouling paintings, ironically.

- Cost competition for bottom cleaning services is good but quite often, you get what you pay for: poor service at the lowest price.

- Whenever you plan to have your boat hauled out, have your bottom cleaner do his work but don't tell him about the pending haul-out, especially if he doesn't provide video records of his cleaning work. You can be the judge of his service quality when you see your vessel's bottom exposed on the travel-lift.

Divers

The topic of bottom cleaning by divers is addressed above as a separate section because of its importance. Below are listed other services that should be performed by trained divers (or a highly capable owner or crewmember), preferably individuals who are certified and insured for commercial work. Even if you don't have an immediate need for these services, someday you likely will, especially if you progress to a larger vessel.

- Inspection and replacement of zinc anodes. This can be performed by the diver who is conducting bottom cleaning but be sure he/she knows the tricks like using sandpaper to thoroughly clean the metal surfaces before the zincs are applied; a hammer to ensure the ball zincs have their entire inner surface in contact with the shaft before final tightening of the locking screws; etc.

- Cleaning and minor maintenance of the vessel's underwater components of its propulsion system, including the running gear (which typically does not have anti-fouling paint), any bow or stern thrusters, rear-mounted trim tabs, vessel stabilizers, etc.

- Depth transducer and speed log maintenance. Typically cleaning surfaces and securing any wiring that may have come adrift.

- Through-hull intake port cleaning, including raw water intakes for engines, generators, air conditioning cooling water strainers, seawater for toilets, inflow for water makers, etc.

Boat Washing

Many boat owners conduct their own hull cleaning. Others hire individuals or a professional service for cleaning and detailing. If you choose to hire someone, here are some factors that warrant consideration.

- Always take recommendations from other boaters who have observed the work ethic of the person(s) hired.

- Ask the worker to introduce you to other boaters in the marina who hire them regularly.

- Make sure the washer(s) considers the job important rather than just an easy way to make a buck. Many unemployed persons walk the docks looking for work with no relevant experience. The quality of their services will correlate with their short resume.

- Don't hire the kids who are often on their cell phones, smoking or taking selfies while they're supposed to be 'on the clock'. Although their hourly rate may be low, their productivity more than negates the investment.

- Look for washers who know the best cleaning agent for each part of the job. Because the work involves glass, fiberglass, metal, teak, painted surfaces, canvas, lines of different materials, nylon covers, etc., experienced personnel often know little tricks. Good cleaning personnel normally bring a whole assortment of products they use regularly. No single cleaning product works for all materials. Anyone who shows up with none should be sent away immediately.

- Furthermore, purchasing only the products from the cleaning shelf of a single marine megastore proves the worker's inexperience and often wastes lots of your money. For instance, liquid dishwasher soap is a better cleaner for teak decks than most products ten times more expensive.

Engine Mechanics

When you arrive in a new area, first check with your marina to determine whether they have skilled engineers and technicians for your engine types. If not, go online, find a local marine service directory or use the Yellow Pages to locate the nearest certified marine repair company for your engine and generator manufacturer. Always ask other boaters with the same engine type for their recommendation on who provides the best engine service. Don't wait until a problem arises. Additionally, this will be your source for engine parts and consumable supplies (e.g., filters, impellors, etc.)

After you have made a tentative choice, visit the service company, register your boat as an account if possible and discuss any discount terms such as eliminating transit costs if work on your vessel goes beyond the first four hours. Next, have one of their technicians come to your vessel to perform an hour or two of basic preventative maintenance. You'll quickly learn about his work ethic, cleanliness, time keeping (e.g., do they charge for transit time to and from their facility?), technical value of his recommendations, etc. If you like this technician's work, request him/her when other work needs to be performed on your vessel because he already has familiarity with your vessel's engine room access, layout and equipment. If the service company cannot commit to sending the same technician for each service call, this should be viewed as a significant disadvantage for you and your budget because the learning curve will begin each time a new technician arrives.

Although there may be a certified engine dealership with full service capabilities in your area, there are times when an independent mechanic is better than a technician from the dealer's representative. Quite often, the independent mechanic has more capabilities than new technicians at the dealership. Because of his proven skills, the independent mechanic often has no shortage of work from existing happy clients and/or referrals. His rate is often substantially less (say $80 per hour versus $120) than the dealership's hourly rate for a less-skilled technician.

A good, independent engine mechanic is worth his weight in gold, especially if he provides his cell phone number in the event you have an engine emergency. Don't abuse this privilege by calling about minor problems that can wait for a weekday and during normal working hours.

Navigation and Electronics Technicians

Today's recreational vessels are equipped with complex electronics systems, including but not limited to navigation, radar, depth and fish finding equipment, sonar electronics, communications, audio-visual, satellite TV, cell phone and Wi-Fi. Best strategies for identifying skilled technicians for maintenance of these diverse systems depend upon whether you're purchasing new equipment or servicing existing components.

SERVICE

When it comes to anything electronic, realize that in today's world almost nothing gets repaired. In most cases, major components are either returned to the factory for repair or replacement under warranty, or they are replaced at the owner's expense with new, upgraded equipment. For example, if a computer chip or 20-cent resistor is blown inside a complex electronic unit, the labor cost for troubleshooting and repair, added to the cost for shipping of the replacement part will most likely exceed the cost of a new system. Yes, a 20-cent component can cause you to buy a new system altogether.

Before you start buying new equipment, there's one more option: Craigslist.org (CL). This free and efficient sales website is the ultimate online Yard Sale for used equipment, even marine. Quite often, boaters purchase new electronics equipment via normal sales outlets then sell their used gear on CL with the result that cost-conscious boaters can (and do) purchase operable equipment at ten to thirty cents on the dollar. Look first on CL if you're not keen on purchasing new equipment at retail prices.

Planned obsolescence seems to be getting shorter — maybe two or three years before the next technological breakthrough. If your electronic component is older than a few years, think seriously about replacement if it starts to malfunction; any older than that and the manufacturer may not support your product.

Given this climate of rapid technological advances, the verb 'Service' would best be defined as the two-step process of troubleshooting then making a decision on whether or not to replace. Having a technician fix the unit is generally not an option. Consequently, for most of your equipment problems, you need a fast and highly experienced electronics troubleshooter who can assess all of your electronics woes. This person often is independent and purposely not a manufacturer's representative. If you find him/her via recommendations of other boaters, they'll be very busy but worth the wait.

Some of these troubleshooters can also recommend the best state-of-the-art replacement technologies but don't limit your options to this one source of information.

PURCHASING NEW ELECTRONICS

If your situation does require purchase of new electronics equipment, regardless of the type or use, here are my recommendations and sequential order:

1. Visit dealer showrooms of the leading manufacturers. Speak with the dealer's salesperson (their technicians preferably) to learn as much as possible about the features of their newest equipment lines. Obtain written price quotations for a few appealing units.

2. Go online and find the website of the same manufacturer and read about the specifications of the newest items to verify what the salesperson had stated. Obtain a price from the website if possible.

3. Go online again, searching for reviews of the equipment you are considering for purchase. Preferably, find reviews that compare similar technologies of numerous manufacturers.

4. Consult with your electronics technician to determine whether he agrees with your choice for the new electronics and that it does not pose any compatibility problems with other integrated systems aboard your vessel.

5. Search on Amazon.com and eBay.com for the specific item you already have other price quotations for. Determine the lowest price online, including taxes and shipping costs. Then evaluate the quality of that supplier to be sure it is a reputable source of new equipment. Do not buy the item yet.

6. Determine whether there is a major boat show or sporting goods convention in your area and in time for your purchasing needs. If so, you can often negotiate a substantial (i.e., 25 percent) discount off retail prices with the dealer's representative at the show. This may be less than the price you have found on Amazon or eBay but possibly not, as online shopping is often the best source for low-cost purchasing.

If you follow this step-wise process, you'll be confident you've found the best deal possible for the item of your choice.

COMPASS CALIBRATION

Any time a new compass is installed on a vessel or when new electronic components are mounted in close proximity to a compass or autopilot heading sensor, the compass must be calibrated. For owners who are not familiar with the process of 'swinging a compass', it is wise to hire an experienced technician for this relatively simple but critical calibration procedure.

Other Maintenance Personnel

In addition to the engine mechanics and electronics experts mentioned above, the boat owner will surely need the services of other skilled marine technicians, including those with expertise in marine plumbing, hydraulics, fiberglass repair, woodworking, anchor windlasses, davits, air conditioning, water making, battery chargers and inverter systems, security systems, etc. Most marinas have a list of recommended local sources for such repair services. Additionally, if the coastal town or city supports an active boating community, local directories of marine service providers and suppliers abound. Fellow boaters in a marina enjoy providing rave reviews about their service technicians but first be sure the boat owner is capable of recognizing good service from bad, especially for your complex onboard systems.

On-Shore Necessities

LOCAL STORAGE FACILITIES

If you plan to live aboard your vessel while berthed in a marina, it is unlikely you'll be able to keep all of your belongings aboard, especially if you have a wife, partner and/or children. Some marinas lease small storage units but rarely are they large enough (say 10-foot by 10-foot floor area) for storage of household items or a small vehicle. Consequently, on-shore storage options are essential for many live-aboard boaters. In most areas clean, secure storage units can be leased from multiple sources and proximity to your marina is typically a key criterion for your selection. As you are evaluating options, note that some facilities have trucks that can be borrowed for transporting your belongings to and from the marina.

AIRPORT

If you select a marina that offers resort amenities and/or is situated in a highly desirable location or climate, it's likely you will have family and friends visit. Similarly, if your vessel is a fine yacht with spare staterooms, they will come from near and far. Surely you will offer to shuttle them to and from the airport so you had better consider the proximity to a good domestic or international airport when selecting a marina or general vicinity. Having to drive 3 hours each way to an international airport is less than optimum.

MARINE HARDWARE STORES

All boaters frequently need assorted items of stainless steel hardware, boat cleaning products, filters, impellors, etc., for basic maintenance and problem solving. If the marina has a ship's store, minor items can be purchased but boaters frequently need stores such as West Marine and Home Depot, which are easy to locate online or via phone searches. Marina personnel can easily identify local independent hardware stores and marine supply sources. Of course, online purchases can often yield good prices but the time delay for shipping often precludes this purchase option versus local shopping.

PROPANE GAS

Many vessels use bottled propane gas for cook stoves, outdoor grills and some lights. Marina personnel can provide local sources.

OTHER COMMON NEEDS

Close proximity of banks, grocers, liquor stores, barbers, hair salons and other essential services will make marina living easy.

• CHAPTER 9 •

The Sea Around Us

Marina Location Versus Regional Physiography

When evaluating a marina in a coastal region, take time to assess its location versus the overall regional physiography (land-based topographic relief, geographic orientation of the coast, bathymetry of inshore and offshore areas, etc.). All of these physical characteristics can have a major impact on your boating experiences as well as conditions within your marina. This is especially important if you are moving to a new region so beware of your new surroundings (and potential hazards). For example, three marina settings are compared below:

COASTAL

If the marina is located on the coast and with only partial barriers for waves entering from offshore, consider the following advantages and disadvantages for this type of marina:

Coastal Marina Advantages and Disadvantages	
ADVANTAGES	**DISADVANTAGES**
• Quick access to the sea • Closer to offshore fisheries • Likelihood of better water quality and clarity at the marina • Lower probability of nuisance algae than in a protected area with minimal flushing • More aquatic and avian marine life	• Potential for large waves and surge from storms • Possibility of dangerous vessel traffic from commercial vessels • Potentially higher Vessel Insurance costs • Accelerated marine growth causing bottom fouling • Higher salinity to accelerate galvanic corrosion • More aquatic and avian marine life

RIVER

If the marina is situated on the bank of a river or within the East Coast Intracoastal Waterway, other conditions are encountered:

River Marina Advantages and Disadvantages	
ADVANTAGES	**DISADVANTAGES**
• Lower marina prices than at coastal facilities	• Greater distance to the sea and saltwater fisheries
• Better protection from coastal storms and waves	• Large wakes from passing ships and barges
• Reduced biofouling and galvanic corrosion in relatively fresh water	• Potential for higher surge during major storms
• Possibly closer access to boatyards and marine repair facilities	• Fresh or brackish water with lower water quality
	• Potentially more exposure to manmade air pollution, noise, odors, light, etc.
	• Bridges that can restrict access to harbors and the coast

HARBOR OR EMBAYMENT

The majority of marinas are located within a harbor, cove or bay to provide relatively good protection from the ocean or coastal environment. Depending upon the local water depth, flushing efficiency and sources of manmade pollution, the water quality of the harbor can range from good to poor so there's no guarantee of what you will encounter without investigating the marina yourself. Other characteristics of harbor marinas are typically midway between those given above for Coastal and River locations. Depending upon which situations are 'show-stoppers' for you, visual assessment is likely necessary for comparison.

Offshore Sea Conditions

If a boater is considering using his/her vessel in unfamiliar territory, it is very important to investigate the ocean environment outside of the harbor, via reading about local boating activity as well as visiting NOAA websites to monitor local weather forecasts and offshore buoy conditions, and study historic wave and wind climatology. The importance of this can be explained through a simple case study: An East Coast boater moves to a town on the central California coast. On the first windless day he launches his 18-foot center-console boat. Venturing out of the harbor, he encounters 10-foot breaking swell at the channel entrance, nearly capsizing his boat when turning back; certainly a tough way to learn about California's long-period swell, often in the absence of local winds.

Similarly, boaters need to develop familiarity with typical sea conditions outside of harbors before they make final decisions on vessel purchases and their intended marina. Boaters who are new to the ocean or others who are considering a larger vessel for a live-aboard lifestyle must become aware of local sea conditions that can adversely impact their experiences, or worse.

In the section named "Weather and Storm Forecasts" in Chapter 10, an extensive list is provided of government and commercial websites for weather, wave, tide and storm forecasts and real-time data dissemination. Boaters should determine which websites are most informative for his/her region and keep 'tuned-in' at all times. Even if you aren't planning a day on the water, your property is at risk when storms approach your marina.

Offshore Fishing Activity

When boaters move to a new marina and/or harbor they must learn about the types of recreational and commercial fishing that is conducted in the region, as well as state fishing laws and regulations. This is important because fishing activity can pose significant hazards to vessel traffic depending upon the type of fishing equipment and procedures used. Examples are given below but there certainly are many types that are not mentioned here.

- Fixed and drifting gill nets are permitted in certain areas. Surface buoys are used to mark the ends of the fishing nets and lights should be used during night but not all fishermen abide by these regulations. Consequently, boaters should know how to identify such nets and anticipate which horizontal direction the gear is oriented so their vessel's props keep well clear of such fishing nets and buoy lines.

- Long-line fishing involves baited hooks on short leaders attached to a strong, primary line that can extend for a quarter-mile or longer. Anchors keep the 'long line' stationary and surface buoys are used to mark the ends. If additional surface-marker buoys are not distributed along the line, vessels may unintentionally cross the fishing gear and become tangled.

- Aquaculture areas are typically stationary and well marked to prevent boaters from interfering with submerged nets and/or vertical arrays for shellfish growth.

- Weirs are long vertical nets oriented perpendicular to shore for redirecting all passing fish into a circular type of net 'bowl' where they are unable to find a way to escape for the 6- to 12-hour time period before the fisherman returns to retrieve the catch from his/her net. The weirs are always anchored in the same location and typically marked on local nautical charts, although they may not be deployed year-round. These large (sometimes a mile long) fishing contraptions have very heavy wire and surface buoys that if tangled with a vessel's keel or running gear can become a major problem. Boaters must stay clear of weirs during daylight and darkness.

- Fish, lobster and crab traps have surface buoys tethered to one or more traps on the bottom. The line beneath the buoy is often slack with the result that considerable line can accumulate just below the surface and foul propellers of vessels that pass close to the buoys. In some regions, multiple traps can be attached to a single ground line with a vertical section of line at each end and marker buoys at the two ends. If a vessel becomes fouled with one of these multiple-trap assemblies, it can be very difficult to haul up enough line to create slack for untangling or cutting.

- Purse seiners are large fishing vessels that move in a circle when deploying a long vertical net around a school of surface fish that has been targeted for capture. Quite often, a small boat (tender) is attached to the end of net and deployed at the start of the process. When the large vessel circles around and links up with the tender, the net is closed and tightened to make a 'purse' that captures the fish inside. These vessels can work by day or night and must be given a wide berth by boaters because they move rapidly and use heavy, dangerous equipment.

- Trawling vessels tow large nets or bottom dragging equipment to catch fish or clams. They typically travel in a straight path for hours, then turn and steam quickly to wash their fishing nets before hauling in to remove their catch. They cannot maneuver well with the trawled gear deployed behind. Consequently, boaters should give trawlers a wide berth.

- Trolling vessels typically use rod and reel equipment during fishing charters with small groups of fishermen aboard. Fishing lines extend behind the trolling vessels, with lures and bait at or near the surface. Boaters must keep far from these fishing vessels to prevent cutting their trolling lines. Most importantly, when they are catching a 'big game' fish, they may have up to a half mile of line out and be showing a white flag with a blue fish on it. Keep far away from these busy fishing vessels.

- Moored and drift fishing vessels may be small or large, with dozens of fishermen aboard. Their lines are typically vertical so they represent a minimal hazard to cruising.

- Dive boats, regardless of size or numbers of scuba divers, must show a red and white 'Diver Down' flag at all times that divers are in the water. Boaters must keep at least 100 yards from such vessels for safety of divers who may be on the surface or rising from depths and unaware of passing vessels.

Anchored Obstructions and Eyesores

When selecting a marina, having a pleasant view of the nearby sea- or landscape is important, although it's less significant than many other features addressed herein. Assuming you only live once, who doesn't want to see the sunset and occasional Green Flash from the cockpit of their vessel every evening while tied securely in your slip? It is possible at some locations.

The worst case is when you sign a marina tenant agreement at a facility with wonderful views of the harbor and city skyline but soon discover that a three-year construction project is about to begin next to your marina. Tall cranes, loud pile-drivers, barges, tug boats and large trucks will all be working six days per week with no noise restrictions. Such projects do occur, often to the marina tenant's surprise.

Similarly, yearlong dredging projects can begin very close to marinas, with tenants having no say about the unsightly dredges and pipes, or the loud noise and diesel fumes that waft downwind from the working equipment. Yes, the

channel dredging is necessary but your views and quality of marina life surely will be affected.

If you're already a marina tenant when these construction projects begin, there's nothing you can do about it. But if you're assessing which local marina would provide best dockage for your vessel, be sure to inquire about any major construction that would be within view of the marina. Honest marina managers will explain what's on the construction schedule, if anything, and they might offer a discount on your slip rate as is customarily done at hotels which are under construction. Negotiate as best you can before you sign a tenancy agreement.

Wave Conditions in the Marina

All marinas have an opening for access to the sea and depending upon the width and geographic orientation of the opening, waves can enter, either directly from the sea or simply from across the harbor. If the harbor is wide, strong winds can generate moderate-sized waves even though the 'fetch' is limited. The worst case is where a marina is situated at the coast or on the shore of a large bay and its opening directly faces the sea with unlimited fetch. Large waves from storms can enter the marina and cause major damage to piers and vessels.

Inexperienced boaters might look at the exposed type of marina favorably because it offers nice views and quick access to the ocean. Experienced boaters typically stay away from these marinas altogether. A telltale sign of whether a marina is severely impacted by large offshore waves is the location of existing boats. If none are close to the opening, there is a good reason, but even those berthed around the corner will be bashed by large waves that enter the marina, bounce off solid walls and create a confused sea farther in.

• AUTHOR RECOMMENDATION •

Assess the exposure of a marina to seas from offshore. Also learn the prevailing wind conditions to determine whether a marina will be choppy most of the boating season, even in the absence of storms.

Bridges and Other Navigation Restrictions

Major U.S. rivers and the Intracoastal Waterway (ICW) along the U.S. East Coast are well traveled by vessels of all sizes. Relatively small power vessels with low vertical profiles and small sailboats with low masts can transit beneath most bridges of rivers and the ICW with ease, also negating the need for bridge  openings. Larger vessels of both categories require bridge openings for passage and many of which are prescheduled versus opening on demand.

Owners of large vessels must be cognizant of all bridges in the vicinity and their schedules for opening. Marinas that are seaward of bridges therefore are more desirable for large vessels versus those that will require the vessel to abide by scheduled bridge openings for outbound and inbound passage.

The significance of marina location versus low bridges is even greater if the marina is located up a river with numerous low bridges that require opening for vessel passage. For some marinas located up major rivers in Florida, vessels must request four or more bridges to open for their passage, before they reach the ICW — a river transit of nearly an hour each way. Boaters must consider this predictable delay if they choose one of the marinas located far up river. Furthermore, transiting the heavily trafficked rivers can be stressful and potentially dangerous for inexperienced boaters. The same situation occurs in rivers of other metropolitan areas around the nation.

Commercial Vessel Traffic

Marinas differ with regard to their proximity to commercial vessels and this can result in noise, privacy and safety problems at some locations. Examples are given below:

CHARTERED FISHING BOATS

Many marinas permit chartered fishing boats to conduct public business from their piers. While fishing is enjoyable for many and it is exciting to see the day's catch come ashore, there can be a few disadvantages of having chartered vessels near your slip:

- Noise from vessels starting engines for early morning charters

- Foot traffic, noise and lack of privacy from public patrons on the docks

- Sometimes noisy crew from fishing boats, celebrating at day's end

- Gulls, pelicans or other sea birds flocking around boats and fish-cleaning tables

If possible, request a slip some distance down the dock from such fishing boats.

SIGHTSEEING VESSELS, FERRIES AND WATER TAXIS

Most city marinas and some private facilities allow commercial vessels to lease slips for various types of tourist business. All involve large numbers of persons congregating on the adjacent docks and consuming nearby parking spaces. It is recommended that boaters who like privacy and security be aware of any potential commercial ventures at the marina they are considering tenancy. Furthermore, some of these waterborne businesses are seasonal and could be inactive when you first visit a marina. Ask marina management and local boaters if boating activity increases significantly during the busy season, and why. Also, look for signs that suggest commercial marine enterprises flourish during certain months.

COAST GUARD, BORDER PATROL, FIRE AND POLICE VESSELS

While it is typically advantageous to have a police presence near your home or vessel, it is best if their docks are not close to yours on account of vessel noise, especially during the night. Take note of berthing areas for municipal vessels when you are viewing a marina.

NAVAL VESSELS

In many large harbors, U.S. naval vessels have a significant presence and their speeding security vessels are vigilant about keeping channels free of recreational traffic during times of naval vessel passage. In harbors that are

home port for submarines, aircraft carriers and other very large vessels with surveillance technology, it is not uncommon for waterways to be closed altogether for up to 30 minutes on both sides of departure and arrival. This is certainly an inconvenience for casual boaters but it is best to be aware of such potential delays as you plan your boating schedule.

Most importantly, boaters must acknowledge that all naval, federal and municipal patrol vessels have the right of way over all other vessels, both commercial and recreational.

Vessel Traffic Separation Zones

U.S. Coast Guard Rules of the Road (2014) and nautical charts specify Traffic Separation Zones to be used by all vessels as they approach and depart from harbors with extensive commercial and/or naval traffic. Recreational boaters must abide by these rules and determine the location of any Separation Zones, especially if the navigation area is new to him/her. Being uninformed is not an acceptable plea when Coast Guard Patrol boards your vessel because of a violation.

Water Clarity in the Marina

Water clarity is typically a concern when a vessel is making fresh water from seawater by desalination equipment and this occurs only when a vessel is away from a marina for extended periods of times (days to weeks). Highly turbid water can clog raw water intake strainers for engines, generators and air conditioner circulating pumps but this equipment is not run long while a vessel is at the dock.

Consequently, water clarity in a marina is mostly an aesthetic issue but clear water certainly does give the boater a more enjoyable experience at the dock rather than dark, green or highly turbid waters, even if they are pollution-free. When evaluating marinas, note that it's not uncommon for water clarity to vary considerably among marinas in the same harbor or general vicinity, especially those close to rivers or shallow bays that are prone to high concentrations of suspended sediment. Algal blooms and Red Tides typically occur during warm months when water temperatures are elevated.

CHAPTER 10

Storm Considerations

This chapter addresses potential storm impacts on your vessel. With a rudimentary education of storm surge, tsunamis and lightning, the informed boater can prevent many problems for his/her vessel. To test your knowledge, consider each of the following questions then revisit them after you have read this chapter:

- Is your vessel at financial risk during storms?

- Where can you access the best forecasts of an approaching storm?

- Do you understand storm-induced vertical surges in water level?

- Are your marina and vessel at significant risk from tsunamis?

- Do you know the common types of damage from lightning?

- What are the best means of securing your vessel for a storm?

- Should you leave your vessel in the water during a major storm?

Evaluate Your Vessel Insurance Terms

All boaters should review the terms of his/her vessel insurance policy before the storm season. Although it may be too late to make changes to the Terms or increase coverage, the owner should at least be cognizant of any storm-related deductibles and limitations in the policy. Some of the key clauses to investigate are indicated below:

NAVIGATION LIMITS

The policy may specify geographic areas that are excluded from the basic insurance coverage during the storm season. In other words, if you cruise in the excluded area, your vessel is not covered. One example, for a Florida vessel cruising during the hurricane season is stated as such, "Vessel is not warranted south of the Tropic of Cancer between June 1 and November 15 inclusive."

PERSONAL NEGLIGENCE

If the owner/operator of the vessel demonstrates negligence in:

- Navigation of the vessel or

- Knowledge of vessel operations, coverage may be negated

This may come into play if the owner chooses to move the vessel away from the dock during a storm, even if the dock is deemed unsafe at the time. If damage to the vessel is incurred while idling around the harbor during the storm, the owner may be deemed negligent for moving off.

SEPARATION OF EQUIPMENT

If insured vessel equipment is removed from the vessel and stored ashore during a storm, even if for protection, some policies insure those items only to 50 percent coverage if damaged or lost. Ironically, they would be 100 percent covered if left aboard the vessel and lost during a storm.

NAMED WINDSTORM

In today's insurance world, coverage varies depending upon whether a storm is 'named' by the National Weather Service. Named storms are so designated because of their intensity regardless of location at-sea or on-land. Most commonly, deductible values are greater for named storms, probably because of the greater financial liability/exposure for insurance companies.

PARTIAL OR TOTAL SUBMERSION

Some policies will not cover claims on a vessel that has become partially or totally submerged while unattended for seven or more days (e.g., abandoned in the eyes of the insurance company). However, if damage and subsequent submergence occurs during heavy weather, your vessel may be covered under the policy so take time to understand your policy.

POLLUTION COVERAGE

Most policies cover damages and costs associated with accidental release of pollutants but be sure vessel damage due to storms is considered 'accidental'.

Other limitations in coverage associated with storms may be imbedded in your vessel insurance policy so review it carefully.

Weather and Storm Forecasts

Keeping abreast of forecasted weather and sea conditions is the most important aspect of boating. Around year 1900 when my Great-Grandfather was stationed aboard the Pollock Rip Lightship east of Cape Cod, Massachusetts, there were no marine weather forecasts. Marconi made the first trans-Atlantic Morse code transmission in 1901, albeit a single letter 'S'. Commercial radio broadcasts began in the U.S. in 1909 but weather forecasts to remote locations came decades later.

Regardless, receiving word that a Nor'easter was bearing down on their anchored lightship was often 'deadly' news if the notice came within hours of storm arrival. Fortunately, Benjamin was not lost at sea or the author would not have been conceived. Many other lightships and their crew were however, lost by capsizing at anchor during winter storms off the U.S East Coast.

Today's boaters are extremely fortunate to have the Internet for dissemination of real-time marine weather data and forecasts. Ironically there's so much information on the web that a novice can often get lost in a cyber sense. Below are provided links to excellent websites and weather forecasting services.

GOVERNMENT WEBSITES FOR MARINE FORECASTING

The U.S. Government has numerous civil and military agencies that generate and disseminate meteorological and oceanographic data to the interested public. Many of their websites allow users to generate tabular and graphic products relevant to their personal marine applications. Recreational and commercial boaters would probably agree on one aspect of the government websites, "There are too many of them." These sites are frequently cross-linked, which sounds efficient, but users are often uncertain whether they're using the best web portal to obtain the most timely and accurate data and forecasts.

Below are identified useful NOAA and Navy websites for accessing meteorological and oceanographic information. The author has little doubt this list is incomplete, even at the time of publication.

Government Websites for Marine Forecasting	
National Ocean Service • Descriptive information and pointers to other NOAA websites for data	www.oceanservice.noaa.gov
National Data Buoy Center • Buoy and Ship Observations	www.ndbc.noaa.gov
National Weather Service • Forecasts	www.weather.gov

NWS Marine Forecasts www.nws.noaa.gov/om/marine/home.htm	
Marine text forecasts and products	
Coastal & Great Lakes weather forecasts	www.nws.noaa.gov/om/marine/zone/usamz.htm
Offshore weather forecasts	www.nws.noaa.gov/om/marine/zone/wrdoffmz.htm
High Seas weather forecasts	www.nws.noaa.gov/om/marine/zone/hsmz.htm
Point weather forecasts	www.nws.noaa.gov/om/marine/point.htm
Predicted Tides and Currents	www.tidesandcurrents.noaa.gov

Observations	
Buoy, C-Man, Ships, Drifter, Gliders, etc.	www.ndbc.noaa.gov
PORTS	www.tidesandcurrents.noaa.gov/ports.html
Gulf Stream and Sea Surface Temperatures	www.opc.ncep.noaa.gov/sst/newSST/GOES_SST.shtml
Tides and Water Levels	www.tidesandcurrents.noaa.gov

NOAA NOWCOAST
www.nowcoast.noaa.gov

Web Mapping Portal to Real-Time Coastal Observations and NOAA Forecasts

- Observations - In-Situ Stations
- Observations – Remote Sensors
- Analyses (Meteorologic and Oceanographic)
- Model Nowcast/Forecast Guidance
- Hazard Advisories, Watches, Warnings
  Short Duration Warnings (floods, thunderstorms, winds, tornadoes)
  Tropical Cyclone Track Forecast (hurricanes)
- Forecasts – Gridded (National Digital Forecast Database)
- Geo-Referenced Links

National Center for Environmental Prediction www.ncep.noaa.gov	
Climate Prediction Center	www.cpc.ncep.noaa.gov
Environmental Modeling Center	www.emc.ncep.noaa.gov
National Hurricane Center • Atlantic • Eastern Pacific	www.nhc.noaa.gov
Ocean Prediction Center	www.opc.ncep.noaa.gov
Marine Weather • Atlantic Products • Pacific Products • Alaska/Arctic Products	www.opc.ncep.noaa.gov/marine_weather.shtml or www.nws.noaa.gov/om/marine
Ocean Products • Sea Surf Temp	www.opc.ncep.noaa.gov/Ocean-Prod_tab.shtml
Coastal Guidance • Storm Surge Models	www.opc.ncep.noaa.gov/coastal_guidance.shtml
Probabilistic Guidance	www.opc.ncep.noaa.gov/probabilistic_guidance.shtml
Environmental Prediction Guidance	www.opc.ncep.noaa.gov/env_prediction_guidance.shtml
Storm Prediction Center • Severe Thunderstorm Watch • Tornado Watch	www.spc.noaa.gov
Weather Prediction Center	www.wpc.ncep.noaa.gov

Center for Operational Oceanographic Products and Services http://co-ops.nos.noaa.gov or www.tidesandcurrents.noaa.gov	
Tidal Predictions	http://co-ops.nos.noaa.gov/tide_predictions.html
Water Levels	http://co-ops.nos.noaa.gov/stations.html?type=Water+Levels
Meteorological Observations	http://co-ops.nos.noaa.gov/stations.html?type=Meteorological%20Observations

Great Lakes Environmental Research laboratory www.glerl.noaa.gov
• Water Levels • Currents • Water Quality • Real-time Meteorological Observations

NOAA Tsunami Website www.tsunami.noaa.gov	
West Coast & Alaska Tsunami Warning Center (WC/ATWC)	wcatwc.arh.noaa.gov
Pacific Tsunami Warning Center (PTWC)	ptwc.weather.gov

Naval Oceanography Portal www.nlmoc.navy.mil/oceanography	
Fleet Numerical Meteorology & Oceanography Center	www.nlmoc.navy.mil/FNMOC
Oceanography Products • Wave Predictions • Sea Surface Temperature	

COMMERCIAL MARINE WEATHER FORECASTING SERVICES

Numerous commercial organizations offer weather services for U.S. coastal regions and offshore. All have websites for presentation of graphic displays and text information. Many of the sites provide quick, easy access to free real-time data from coastal weather stations and buoys that are maintained by U.S. government organizations and universities with marine observation programs.

While some of the providers of weather data post free information and forecasts, others require users to pay for weather forecasting and vessel routing services, typically at monthly subscription rates.

The alphabetized list provided below identifies many of the prominent commercial online weather services available in the U.S. The list is likely to have omissions, which are unintended. Note also that this list purposely does not include firms that only provide user access to weather data compiled and/or forecasted by other organizations.

Commercial Online Weather Services	
www.accuweather.com	AccuWeather • Forecasts
www.boatus.com	Boat US • Forecasts • Hurricane tracking
www.buoyweather.com	BuoyWeather • Forecasts • Real-time buoy data • Tides
www.captainsweather.com	Captain's Weather • Forecasts
www.commandersweather.com	Commander's Weather • Forecasts
www.globalsailingweather.com	Global Sailing Weather • Forecasts – Global
www.mwxc.com	Marine Weather Center • Forecasts – Caribbean and East Coast
www.oceanweather.com	Ocean Weather Inc. • Forecasts • Real-time buoy data
www.passageweather.com	Passage Weather • Forecasts and routing • Gulf Stream • Tropical warnings

Commercial Online Weather Services	
www.stormsurf.com	Storm Surf • Weather and surf forecasts and modeling • Real-time buoy data
www.weather.com	Weather.com • Forecasts • Severe weather
www.weatherguy.com	Weather Guy • Forecasts and routing • Tropical cyclones • Tsunami warnings
www.wriwx.com	Weather Routing Inc. • Forecasts and routing
www.wunderground.com/marine-weather	Weather Underground • Forecasts • Real-time buoy data • Wave heights • Hurricanes and tropical cyclones • Sailing weather

Storm Surge

Major storms impact all coastlines of the U.S. In the Pacific Northwest, storms from the Gulf of Alaska send huge swell and high winds to southeast Alaska and the Pacific coast of Washington, Oregon and California. In New England, intense Nor'easters have central pressures that can drop rapidly ('bomb') and generate very large swell and storm surge that destroy coastal property.

The most severe coastal storms in the U.S. are undoubtedly hurricanes (tropical and extra-tropical cyclones) characterized by large horizontal scales and very low central pressures. Their high winds and waves cause tremendous damage to property but the storm surge flooding associated with hurricanes is responsible for the majority of damage and loss of life. Examples are the Galveston, Texas hurricane of 1900 with surge over 18 feet and Katrina in 2005 with 25-foot surge on the coast of Mississippi (Needham and Keim, 2011).

Recent studies at the NOAA National Hurricane Center (J. Rhome, 2013) and other modeling facilities (Resio and Westerink, 2008; Needham and Keim, 2011) have advanced our knowledge of storm surge associated with hurricanes. Additionally, numerical models of surge prediction have proven that a variety of geographic, meteorological and oceanographic factors effect surge, including:

- Physical size of the storm

- Air pressure in the central eye of the storm

- Intensity of the wind field

- Persistence of hurricane-force winds at the coast

- Rate of storm movement

- Angle of storm track toward the coastline

- Water depth in the coastal area

- Shape of the coastline and local embayments

- Land topography or obstacles to surge propagation

- Run-off from rainfall

- Tide levels during storm passage

In simple terms, as a hurricane moves toward a coastline (typically in a westerly or northerly direction in the Gulf of Mexico or along the East Coast), onshore winds in the northeast quadrant of the counter-clockwise rotating storm push surface waters toward shore. If the coastal waters are shallow and the rate of storm advance is slow, significant volumes of water can pile up at the coast. If the advancing surge (pile of water) is blocked and trapped as within an embayment, the local water level will rise sharply and rainfall run-off from land into the water can add to the flooding. As the center of the storm passes over the now-flooded area, the low atmospheric pressure of the storm's center allows the underlying waters to bulge upward (described as the inverse-barometer effect) as much as 1 to 3 feet depending upon the pressure in the eye of the storm (see table below).

Hurricanes			
Hurricane Category	Min. Atmospheric Pressure (Mb)	Surface Rise From Low P (Ft)	Estimated Total Surge (Ft)
1	980	1.1	4 - 5
2	972	1.4	6 - 8
3	955	1.9	9 - 12
4	932	2.7	13 - 18
5	918	3.1	> 18

Thus, the atmospheric-induced rise in water level can constitute from 15 to 25 percent of the total surge experienced; the remainder is due to strong winds piling up water at the shoreline.

Additionally, the normal tides also cause temporal variability in water level and if the time of maximum storm surge corresponds with the time of the high tide, you have very high water locally. In the Gulf of Mexico where tidal ranges are generally less than 2 feet, the tidal contribution to maximum surge is moderate. In New England however, when a hurricane hits landfall at the time of high tide (possibly 5 feet above mean water level) the additive effects of surge and tide can be catastrophic. The best case (e.g., least coastal damage) is when a hurricane hits landfall at the time of low water and the surge is partially offset by the tidal depression in sea level.

Tsunamis

Tsunamis are rare marine wave events that can cause major havoc to coastal areas and cause numerous fatalities as reported worldwide during the past two decades. Meaning 'harbor wave' in Japanese, the name originated from fishermen who had gone to sea then returned to encounter destruction from a huge wave that seemed to have been confined to the harbor. Scientists more appropriately named this fascinating marine phenomenon a 'seismic sea wave" in place of tsunami or the equally incorrect but common term 'tidal wave'. The seismic connotation also was wrongly limiting as later discovered that large surface waves could also be created by a variety of natural and manmade events including: earthquakes, volcanic eruptions, landslides, glacier fracturing, meteor impacts, passage of abrupt meteorological storms, underwater explosions or detonations, etc. Tsunamis could result from any of these processes as long as a major displacement of water occurred but not necessarily on the seafloor.

Tsunamis have very long wavelengths and resemble a rapidly rising tide but have periods (times between wave crests of the same event) that range from minutes to hours. Heights of the tsunami wave as it impacts the shore depend upon many physical factors, both at the source and at the point of impact on the shoreline. Tsunamis of a few meters in height are reported by today's media but many past events have been reported with heights of tens of meters; some as high as 50 meters (164 feet). The earliest on record was during 426 B.C. in the Mediterranean.

Damage from a large tsunami can occur in two phases. First, the incoming wall of water can destroy most objects in its path. Second, if the volume of water carried upland is great, additional destruction occurs when the water reverses direction and seeks lower areas. On this ebb flow, tremendous debris is carried out with more destruction resulting, even if the wave height is much less than that of the incoming wall.

Tsunamis generated by earthquakes cannot be accurately predicted even if the epicenter location, depth and magnitude of seismic event are known. Consequently, it is difficult to confidently broadcast early Tsunami Warnings that could impact thousands of citizens in a coastal region. Subsea technology for monitoring sudden changes in sea height (from pressure measurements on the seafloor) is improving, as are systems for transmitting the near-real-time data from distant, mid-ocean sites to shore-based receiving stations and then to tsunami modeling facilities. Cost for deploying the expensive mid-ocean tsunami early warning arrays will likely be the limiting factor for the next two decades.

Tsunamis in the U.S.

Dunbar and Weaver conducted an extensive study of tsunami events in the U.S. published in 2008. The authors accessed NOAA's National Geophysical Data Center (NGDC) that represents a vast archive of earth science data including global observations of tsunami sources and 'run-up' records. More specifically, the database was used to assess tsunamis that impacted the U.S. and its territories, the first being a tsunami event that impacted the Hawaiian coast in the 16th century, killing many inhabitants. A summary of this hazard assessment, based upon over 500 years of data, is shown below.

Tsunamis Hazards in the United States			
Geographic Area	Run-up Events	Reported Deaths	Potential Hazard
US Atlantic Coast	33	0	Very low
US Gulf Coast	1	0	Very low
Puerto Rico & Virgin Islands	48	172	High
US West Coast	550	24	High
Alaska	352	222	Very high
Hawaii	1592	326	Very high

Consistent with sensational news reports during the past decade, historical analyses of tsunamis demonstrate that U.S. coastlines on the Pacific Ocean are high to very high risk, based upon the frequency of tsunami-driven run-up events. The largest tsunami heights occur in Alaska and Hawaii, thus characterizing these areas as very high hazard areas.

For the west coast states of California, Oregon and Washington, the tsunami hazard is high yet less than for Alaska and Hawaii. The frequency of events along our west coast states is low but the magnitude of the earthquakes and tsunamis are very large, resulting in a high hazard characterization.

Puerto Rico and the U.S. Virgin Islands also are characterized as high hazard areas based upon the observed tsunami events. In contrast, U.S. states along the Atlantic and Gulf of Mexico coasts have experienced very few run-up events during the past 200 years, yielding a very low hazard characterization in those regions.

Pacific tsunamis are typically more hazardous than those experienced in the Atlantic and Caribbean because Pacific earthquakes have larger physical dimensions than their eastern counterparts and therefore displace larger volumes of water that then drive the tsunamis.

Fortunately for boaters in the U.S., the technology for tsunami detection and early warning systems has improved greatly during the past decade. Coastal communities in tsunami prone areas also have become more aware of the potential risk of these often catastrophic events. The rapid speed at which tsunamis can impact a harbor plus the associated height of water level rise should be a high concern to all boaters, especially those on Pacific shores and in the Caribbean.

NOAA's Tsunami website (**www.tsunami.noaa.gov**) is an excellent source for warnings, education and learning about the latest developments in tsunami research and monitoring technologies.

Meteo-tsunamis

THE PHYSICS OF METEO-TSUNAMIS

The above discussion about tsunami observations in the U.S. promulgates the conventional belief that tsunamis are generally caused by a subsea seismic event and that coastal regions void of nearby seismic activity are statistically void of tsunamis events. Warning: don't let these statistics give you a false sense of security, especially if you're a boater on the U.S. East Coast or in the Great Lakes. Case in point: in June of 2013 a substantial tsunami impacted the southern coast of New England (Fraser, 2013) and it was later determined that the rapid rise in coastal water level was caused by an intense meteorological storm front (derecho) that quickly moved offshore and across the relatively shallow continental shelf (Bailey et al., 2014). Their analyses and reviews of historic data have shown that meteo-tsunamis are relatively common along the U.S. East Coast and are generated by storm fronts moving either onshore or offshore.

The primary factors in generation of a meteo-tsunami are: 1) the magnitude of the atmospheric pressure fluctuation observed during the short time interval that the weather front passes a particular location (i.e., a 5 mbar increase in atmospheric pressure over 10 minutes), and 2) the speed at which the front passes over the coastal waters. Regarding the speed issue, it's important to first review the basic physics of waves in the ocean. When the height of a wave is sufficiently large that the trough of the wave feels the effect of bottom friction, its horizontal speed is governed by the water depth causing the wave to slow down as it encounters shallower water. For example, a very large wave would travel at 37 miles/hour in water 100 feet deep whereas it would slow to 16 miles/hour when the depth is 20 feet. Consequently, a large seismic-generated tsunami wave would decelerate as it approaches the shoreline and its large mass of water would pile up, as observed for the catastrophic tsunamis reported in recent years.

For meteo-tsunami generation, amazing things happen when the horizontal speed of the atmospheric storm matches the theoretically predicted speed of an ocean wave at the particular water depth. In other words, if you have a storm moving on or offshore (yes, in either direction) at say 25 miles/hour, there's a magic water depth (location on the continental shelf) where the two speeds match. When this occurs and if the atmospheric pressure fluctuation is large (i.e., over 4 mbar) then the effect is similar to dropping a stone into a swimming pool – waves propagate outward from the source location of the short-term atmospheric depression (or relaxation) of the ocean surface.

Interestingly, for a strong storm front (derecho or squall line) passing over the continental shelf, it makes no difference which direction the storm is moving; if substantial meteo-tsunami waves are generated, they will head toward shore, decrease in speed with decreasing water depth and increase in wave height until they encounter the shore.

Tsunami height and coastal inundation are maximized in semi-enclosed bays where the shape, size and depth of the water body are optimum for natural resonance (sloshing, to use a non-scientific term).

By comparing the time lag between passage of the air pressure fluctuation and the time of water level rise at shore-based monitoring stations along the U.S. East Coast, and characterizing the speed and direction of the atmospheric disturbance, Bailey et al., (2014) concluded that the peculiar, observed water level fluctuations in 2013 were due to waves generated at the edge of the continental shelf. Significant local impacts were felt at numerous locations along the New England shore, with a maximum height of 2 feet in Narragansett Bay, RI on account of the shape of the coastline and inshore water depths. Yes, the meteo-tsunami impacts were felt many hours after the atmospheric storm had moved offshore.

Waves from this event also propagated to the east and south with effects detected many hours later as far as Bermuda and Puerto Rico, albeit at smaller amplitudes.

Meteo-tsunami Observations in the U.S.

In addition to the East Coast meteo-tsunami event of 2013, Bailey et al., (2014) have reported additional significant meteo-tsunamis in the U.S. including:

- A 10-foot wave generated by a meteo-tsunami in Lake Michigan in 1954. Subsequently, scientists have determined that Lakes Michigan and Erie are relative 'hot spots' for this meteorological process because of the frequency of intense meteorological fronts passing overhead during summer months and the natural resonance of these enclosed water bodies.

- A 10-foot high meteo-tsunami event impacted Daytona Beach, FL in summer of 1992, later determined to be caused by a squall line which passed north and offshore of the impacted area. There was no local meteorological disturbance to warn the public that such a wave would occur.

- Another meteo-tsunami event occurred in 2008 on the coast of Maine with reported surge heights between 4 and 12 feet caused by a meteorological storm that passed over the continental shelf in the Gulf of Maine.

METEO-TSUNAMI OBSERVATIONS WORLDWIDE

Accessing the National Geophysical Data Center Tsunami Database, which spans from 2,000 B.C. to 2014, Bailey et al., (2014) have developed statistics on the number of tsunamis caused by various generation mechanisms. Globally, 1680 tsunamis were apparently caused by subsea seismic activity compared to 111 by subsea volcanoes and only 32 (3 percent) by meteorological processes. Additionally, a large number of events had unknown sources and many could have been meteo-tsunamis.

To illustrate that major meteo-tsunamis are a worldwide phenomena, a few examples of major events are given below:

- In Japan, where meteo-tsunamis are called "abiki" a major event occurred in 1979 with a wave height of nearly 15 feet. High risk areas are associated with narrow embayments that have favorable resonance geometries which amplify the incoming waves.

- The Spanish coastline in the western Mediterranean Sea also has experienced major meteo-tsunamis, which are locally called "rissaga". One such event occurred in 2006 when a summer storm passed through the region and generated meteo-tsunami waves up to 15 feet high within a harbor whose geometry was resonance-favorable.

- The eastern shore of the Adriatic Sea (in the Italian Mediterranean region) also encounters numerous meteo-tsunamis. Major events occurred in 1978 and 2003, with wave heights of 19 feet for the earlier of the two meteo-tsunamis.

WARNING SYSTEMS FOR METEO-TSUNAMIS

International recognition and acknowledgment of the potential dangers from meteo-tsunamis on coastal communities precedes that within the U.S. For example, in 1984 the Spanish Meteorological Agency initiated a rigassa warning system that issues public warnings based upon forecasted storms which are likely to be favorable for meteo-tsunami generation.

Because of the large area and metropolitan population along the U.S. East Coast, a meteo-tsunami warning system would be difficult and very costly to implement. Regardless, there needs to be better education of the coastal populace and boaters in the U.S. so they understand the meteo-tsunami phenomenon and when they may be at risk of impact.

NOAA meteorologists and physical oceanographers are continually improving their numerical models of meteo-tsunamis and in recent years, have made significant advancements with identification of storms that are favorable to meteo-tsunami generation. All boaters, especially those on the East Coast and Great Lakes should keep aware of the latest developments in this realm of marine science.

Surge Effects in a Marina

Knowledge of the physical processes that govern storm surge and tsunamis is essential for coastal boaters. An uninformed person would be concerned about how storm winds and waves could affect his/her vessel but totally overlook surge factors, which can be the most dangerous effects of a storm. You can imagine such a boater saying: "Why should I be concerned about my boat, which will rise with the water level, versus my friend's house on the canal that will surely get flooded during the storm"

SURGE CASE 1

Clarence has his boat berthed at a marina near the head of a narrow, pointed bay. The marina piers are well protected from harbor waves and a headland to the east partially blocks winds from the offshore direction. The marina has fixed docks and with a tidal range of only 2 feet, it's easy for Clarence to leave a couple feet of slack on each dock line to facilitate boat movement during tidal fluctuations in water level.

The day before the storm is forecasted to make landfall, Clarence visits the marina to add more dock lines, figuring it's all he needs to do in preparation for the storm. He's surprised, to say the least, when the dockmaster informs him that he must evacuate his boat immediately. The explanation is simple: storm winds will not exceed forty knots at the marina but a 4-foot surge is expected near the time of high water. "From shore, we won't even see the tops of our pilings. Everything will be underwater." says the dockmaster. "At least I don't have to worry about my fixed piers washing up and away. You boaters just need to get your scows out of here, now."

SURGE CASE 2

Fred has his 40-foot trawler berthed at a different marina in the same harbor. He likes the floating piers at his facility because tending of dock lines and his power cord is much easier than for vessels at marinas with fixed docks. Fred hears about the approaching storm and makes plans to haul his boat immediately. At his facility, it's the dockmaster who's fretting because he knows all of his floating piers will ride up their containment pilings then over the top and begin floating horizontally wherever they wish. Most likely they'll all be piled up at one end of the harbor, all broken as scrap lumber. There isn't much he can do, other than hope that the storm slows its advance and arrives closer to the time of low tide. "Please don't go over the tops of my pilings" the dockmaster says to his piers.

SURGE CASE 3

Hurricanes do not impact central California but the local harbormaster received warning that a tsunami of South American origin may impact his harbor in 2 hours. Surge from tsunamis can be even greater than surge generated by hurricanes and typically there is no warning with tsunamis.

A couple hours' notice is good but insufficient time for many vessels to be hauled out of the small California marina. Consequently, boaters can select one of four options:

SURGE CASE 3 (CONTINUED)

1. Watch their vessel from shore,

2. Board their vessel and tend their dock lines in hope that this will prevent any problems,

3. Cast off all dock lines and maneuver the vessel to the center of the harbor and away from any drifting vessel or debris, or

4. Move the vessel out of the harbor altogether and offshore to much deeper water where tsunami-driven water level fluctuations should be smaller.

Via a public announcement, all boaters are informed they cannot exercise option 3 because tsunami-driven currents may become dangerous in the harbor and navigation buoys may be pulled off their moorings. Option 4 is disallowed also, because offshore conditions are unpredictable and if floating debris becomes a major problem in the harbor, vessels may not be permitted to return.

Thus, all boats must remain secured to their piers for the duration of the tsunami event. Some owners choose to board their vessels and watch as the water level rapidly rises up the adjacent piling — 3 feet in 10 minutes actually. Then it drops again, then rises.

SURGE CASE 3 (CONTINUED)

Watching from his office on shore, the dockmaster is ecstatic that this tsunami arrived near the time of low water so his floating piers did not go over the tops of his pilings. If they had, with all boats attached, it would have been a major catastrophe as the water level descended. Some of the floating piers could have become trapped on top of pilings and boats would have been tethered at all angles of disarray, or worse, having hulls impaled on the pilings. When the water level subsided, some boats would have been on their sides and ready for flooding when the tide rose again. Fortunately, this disaster was averted by the natural tide.

• AUTHOR RECOMMENDATION •

If major storm surge is predicted at your marina or harbor, haul your vessel out of the water immediately. There is no other option for protecting your vessel from large storm surge.

Seiches and Slosh in Major Lakes

Seiches (or slosh as they are often called) are large and periodic fluctuations in water level sometimes observed on the U.S. Great Lakes. Although normally generated by the passage of strong atmospheric fronts and winds, local earthquakes also can cause them.

The term seiche originated from the first observation of the phenomenon by a French hydrologist as he witnessed water oscillating back and forth in Lake Geneva, Switzerland in 1890. In a Swiss dialect, the French word seiche means to sway back and forth, a common phenomenon in Alpine lakes where winds can be intense.

The key requirement for seiche generation is that the water body be enclosed or mostly enclosed so large and long waves bounce off both ends of the basin or lake. When strong winds or atmospheric pressure fronts push water from one end of a water body to the other, the water reverses direction as soon as the initial horizontal force is removed. This pile of water may oscillate back and forth for periods of days, manifesting itself as waves that move in opposite directions along the axis of the water body. These opposing waves result in a standing wave with largest variations in water level observed at the two ends of the water body.

In the Great Lakes, the time period between high and low water levels from the seiche can range from 4 to 8 hours. Although somewhat similar in temporal characteristics as coastal ocean tides, seiches have nothing to do with astronomically forced tides in the sea. The frequency of seiche oscillations is determined by the size of the water body, its depth, bottom topography and the water temperature. Lake Erie experiences many seiches, especially when strong winds blow from southwest to northeast along the primary geographic axis of the lake.

The National Weather Service now issues low-water advisories for portions of the Great Lakes when seiches of 2 feet or greater are likely to occur. Historic records show that seiches with very large vertical range have been observed at the ends of most Great Lakes. For example, in 1848 a 22-foot seiche at the east end of Lake Erie killed 78 people and created an ice dam that temporarily stopped the river flow at Niagara Falls. In 1954, a 10-foot seiche on Lake Michigan resulted in eight fishermen drowning.

In 1995, a large seiche on Lake Superior caused the water level to oscillate by 3 feet within 15 minutes and the same storm caused a seiche on Lake Huron with water level fluctuations of 6 feet in two hours.

There is no doubt that boaters and marinas on the Great Lakes need to be aware of the seiche phenomena and best plans for readiness. Preparations for coastal storm surge events, as outlined above, are mostly applicable to seiche events in major lakes.

Lightning

This section provides interesting statistics on lightning reports in the U.S. followed by potential impacts to vessels and recommendations after a strike.

LIGHTNING STATISTICS IN THE U.S.

Because of the severe injuries and death caused by convective storms in the U.S., the National Weather Service has compiled accurate statistics on the incidence of reported lightning casualties since 1959. These interesting data have been reported by a number of authors (Holle, et al., 1999; Curran, et al., 2000; Holle, 2013) with key findings presented below.

In the U.S. over the past 30 years, more persons have died from flooding than from lightning and tornados (these two being about equal) and fewer deaths have been attributed to hurricanes. Lightning casualties are more frequent than those resulting from tornados. The following conclusions have been developed from the national storm database:

- Summer months have the highest number of lightning related deaths, with July being the highest

- Two-thirds of the strike casualties occur between 12 and 4 p.m. local time

- 91 percent of the death events result in a single fatality

- Sunday experiences the most fatalities; 24 percent more than any other day

- Outdoor recreation is associated with most of the lightning fatalities

- Males experience 84 percent of the lightning fatalities (4.6 times females)

- Over the past 35 years there has been a 30 percent decrease in lightning casualties, likely because of improved storm forecasting and public warnings

Florida has experienced twice as many lightning-based casualties than any other state in the U.S. However, when the death statistics are normalized by each state's population Florida ranks fifth in the country. A comparison of lightning fatalities for selected coastal states is given below for the period 1959 to 2012, normalized by state population.

Lightning Deaths in the United States				
State	Deaths	Lightning deaths per Million Residents	Ratio of Residents per Lightning Death	National Rank
Florida	468	0.78	1,282,051	5
Mississippi	105	0.77	1,298,701	6
Louisiana	41	0.65	1,538,462	8
N Carolina	194	0.56	1,785,714	13
Maine	27	0.44	2,272,727	23
Texas	215	0.25	4,000,000	33
Massachusetts	30	0.10	10,000,000	45
California	31	0.02	50,000,000	47
Alaska/HI	0	0.00		

Of all the coastal states, Florida ranks highest in lightning fatalities, with Gulf states being close behind. Florida had 468 fatalities reported in 53 years (8.8 per year). Relatively high air temperatures and frequency of convective storms certainly drive these statistics, as do the popularity of outdoor recreational activity in the country's lowest-latitude state, Florida. In New England and along the West Coast the probability of lightning fatalities is low whereas in Hawaii and Alaska, it is improbable.

· AUTHOR OBSERVATION ·

Being killed by lightning is more likely in low-latitude coastal states than winning a major lottery. Furthermore if you are male, living in Florida and conducting an outdoor recreational activity around 4 p.m. on a Sunday in July, your chances of being struck by lightning are optimized. The good news is that you'll most likely be the only person to die from that lighting strike.

LIGHTNING STRIKES OF VESSELS

Boat US (2010) has compiled statistics on lightning strikes of vessels (not persons) from insurance claims submitted to their organization by their members. While their analysis is not a database of all vessel strikes for the entire nation, it does involve strikes throughout the U.S. for the period 2000 through 2005. Some of the key results from their findings are given below:

- Nationally, the odds of a boat being struck by lightning are about 1.2 in 1,000.

- In Florida however, the strike rate is three times higher and 33 percent of all Boat US lightning claims were in Florida.

- Chesapeake Bay has the second highest incidence of boat strikes at 29 percent.

- The majority of strikes occur on sailboats (4 per 1,000) on account of their tall masts.

- Powerboats are struck less (0.5 per 1,000) but trawlers have the highest number of strikes of all powerboats (2 per 1,000), likely because they have higher antennae and superstructures than smaller vessels, which exist in greatest number.

- Wide, multihull sailboats are struck twice as often as mono-hull sailboats, probably because they are berthed alone rather than beside other vessels which can provide 'shielding' (e.g., act as adjacent targets for lightning).

- Vessels with lower structure and antennae than their neighbors can still be hit directly by lightning so shielding is not a guaranteed deterrent.

Lightning damage to a vessel is often readily apparent from physical damage and/or inoperable electronics. However, there are cases when lightning-damaged wiring or electrical components did not present itself for many years then finally failing or shorting out when least expected, or desired.

• AUTHOR RECOMMENDATION •

The most important action a boater should take following a lightning strike to his/her vessel is to look below decks to determine whether there are any leaks. Lightning must seek a point of exit and this can result in 1) a hole through the hull at any location or 2) damage to a through-hull fitting beneath the water line. In either case, seawater entry can be significant and the vessel can be at risk of sinking. In such cases, immediate repair or haul-out must be conducted.

Even if a leak is not apparent following a major lightning strike to a vessel, it is recommended that the vessel be hauled out for a short time to conduct a thorough visual inspection to identify any potential damage to through-hull fittings, running gear or the hull. With some vessel insurance policies, this type of 'short-haul' for inspection purposes does not have a deductible charge.

The electrical bonding system of the vessel must also be carefully checked following a lightning strike because the high voltage often sacrifices it. Similarly, the vessel's shore power cord and connectors must be checked for damage. Also, all battery charging/inverting systems, batteries, navigation equipment and electronics, fuel tanks, etc.

VESSEL PREPARATION FOR LIGHTNING

Having learned the types of vessel damage that can occur from a lightning strike, some precautions are given below:

- If the vessel is in port, disconnect both ends of the shore power cord (from its pedestal and the vessel) and stow it in a covered area.

- Disconnect all antennae from their electronics components and if possible, move the ends of the wiring away from components.

- Lower antennae as much as physically possible.

- Disconnect other electronic components from main electrical circuits.

- Back up computer data on external storage drives and remove them from the boat.

- Disconnect power supply cords from all computers and stow major components below.

- Disconnect essential VHF and other radio equipment from power sources. Also disconnect the primary batteries of emergency radios until after the storm passes. They may be essential for your safety.

- Have all persons remain below and with as much distance as possible from engines, major metal components, metal rails, etc.

- On sailing vessels, remain as far as possible from winches, metal stays/guy wires and masts.

Dock Lines During Storms

When a major storm approaches, most boat owners begin their preparations by adding more and bigger lines to secure their vessel in its marina slip but this isn't always the best strategy. Step 1 is simple: Meet with the dockmaster because he/she can normally recommend the best actions for safety of your vessel. Factors to be considered include:

- A communication plan for contacting emergency personnel

- Where boaters should go for if they suddenly need shelter

- Learned experience from past storms

- Worst-case surge conditions and What-If strategies

- Which neighboring vessels may pose problems, if unattended

- When to disconnect shore power lines

- Strength of fixed piers and pilings

- Are floating piers safe to secure to?

- Use of chains on piers versus securing to conventional cleats

- Chaffing gear everywhere

- When to abandon ship

• AUTHOR RECOMMENDATION •

Clearly, there are many issues to consider, so your first meeting with the dockmaster should be a week before storm arrival (e.g., before the storm season).

Also note that marinas are responsible for assuring their docks and piers are securely anchored to withstand forces from tropical storms, hurricanes, tsunamis and other acts of nature. Having your vessel attached securely to a pier does little good if the pier will break away from its adjacent piling or anchor, or from its shore connection during the peak of a storm. Ask the dockmaster to explain their hurricane preparedness plan and how often they inspect and replace any 'ground tackle' used to secure their piers. If their Plan can't be clearly explained, assume your vessel will incur major damage when a major storm or tsunami impacts the marina.

Haul-Out and Tie-Down On the Hard

When large storms and hurricanes approach a U.S. coastal region, weather forecasters generally provide good predictions of wind, wave and sometimes, surge conditions. Boaters typically have a few days to evaluate the forecast and decide whether they should haul their vessel out of the water rather than leave it exposed in a marina or on a mooring. Small boats can easily be hauled and taken to shelter on trailers days before storm arrival. However, the larger the vessel the more complicated the situation becomes. For example, some boating areas have very few boatyards with capabilities sufficient to haul large (e.g., greater than 45-foot) vessels and those facili-

ties can get overbooked during approaching storms. If the boat owner does not plan well ahead, he may discover there's no yard that can haul his vessel before the storm – not a comfortable situation.

At higher latitudes such as in New England, the onset of autumn and frequent storms causes many owners to haul their vessel in late August or early September before the storm season (and possible hurricanes) arrives but that constitutes the end of their short boating season, until the following May or June.

Boaters in Florida have a 12-month season so the only time they would haul their vessel is prior to a major tropical storm or hurricane. To reduce pre-storm stress for owners of large boats, some boatyards now offer a hurricane insurance policy whereby if the owner pays an annual fee (in advance), the yard will haul and secure the vessel on the hard in their upland storage lot. This procedure will be implemented for named storms, whether the owner is on-site or not. This gives the owner significant comfort rather than having to worry about the vessel remaining in the water to be damaged by the storm and all contents lost. Additionally, many vessel insurance companies will provide a reduction in fees if the owner shows proof of his hurricane policy. A very good investment for vessels in hurricane-prone regions. Boaters should inquire whether any boatyards in their region offer such insurance policies.

Forced Evacuation of Vessels

The worst case for a boat owner is to have his/her vessel berthed in a marina that insists all vessels evacuate the facility when a major storm approaches. It is the marina's right to impose this severe condition and it will surely be specified in their marina tenant agreement. A boat owner's first reaction might be to attempt removal of this clause from their agreement, but when he/she learns the marina will remove its docks when a major storm is approaching, there's definitely no point in fighting this stipulation.

A wise boat owner will acknowledge that the marina's evacuation policy is based upon real experience with major storms. They know that if your vessel and their piers are left in the water during the storm, they will be damaged or destroyed. Consequently, if the boat owner wishes to be a tenant of that marina, he must have a plan for moving the vessel to a safer marina and/or boatyard for haul-out when a major storm approaches. This sounds extreme but such cases do exist. Those boat owners who don't plan for it would actually be forced to head out to sea searching for another marina. Wouldn't their vessel insurance company be pleased to hear this storm strategy?

CHAPTER 11

Health and Safety

Safety Equipment Provided by the Marina

Boater safety begins at the dock. As soon as your vessel is secured in her slip for the first day of your tenancy, start familiarizing yourself with the safety aids on your dock and nearby marina facilities, especially noting locations of life saving equipment that is discussed below. If any of these are absent from your marina, remind marina management that it is their responsibility to provide these essential safety items.

- Automated External Defibrillator (AED) units are designed to save the life of a person suffering from sudden cardiac arrest. One or more AEDs should be mounted in conspicuous locations at the marina for use by boaters in the event of cardiac emergencies. Familiarization with AED operation is highly recommended for all persons, before an emergency may arise.

- Life rings should be mounted on all major docks and thrown to anyone in the water who needs assistance.

- Vertical ladders should be firmly attached to at least one pier or dock in the vicinity of your vessel. This is especially important on fixed piers because the water level at any given time can be many feet below dock level, thus preventing a person from climbing out of the water following a mishap.

- At some safety conscious marinas, a list is posted of boaters who are trained to administer Cardio-Pulmonary Resuscitation (CPR). A copy of this list with tenant phone numbers is good to have aboard your vessel in the event that CPR assistance is needed.

Emergency Contact List

Boaters must develop an emergency contact list when settling into a new marina or area. Examples of important facilities and agencies are given below. Websites are provided for a few of the national emergency organizations. Speak with your marina to determine local phone numbers for these important organizations.

LOCAL EMERGENCY CONTACTS

- Local Police

- Marina Security

- Fire Department

- Emergency Management/Civil Defense

- Ambulance

- Hospital

- Emergency Medical Clinic

- Emergency Dentist

Marine Emergency Contacts	
Service	**Internet**
U.S. Coast Guard	www.uscgboating.org
Regional Units	www.uscg.mil/top/units
Safety – Accident reporting form	www.uscgboating.org/recreational-boaters/accident-reporting.php
"A Boater's Guide to the Federal Requirements for Recreational Boats"	www.uscgboating.org/images/420.PDF

Vessel Towing Services (private)		
Service	**Phone**	**Internet**
Sea Tow	800-4-SEATOW	www.seatow.com
Boat U.S.	800-889-4869	www.boatus.com/towing

National Emergency Contacts/ Federal Emergency Organizations

Service	Phone	Internet
U.S. Customs and Border Protection	800-232-5378	www.cbp.gov
U.S. Customs and Border Protection Sectors		www.cbp.gov/ border-security/ along-us-borders/ border-patrol-sectors
American Red Cross	800-773-2767	www.redcross.org
Center for Disease Control		www.cdc.gov
Federal Emergency Management Agency	800-621-3362	www.fema.gov
National Hurricane Center		www.nhc.noaa.gov
Environmental Protection Agency		www.epagov
National Oceanic and Atmospheric Administration		www.noaa.gove
National Weather Service		www.nws.gov
National Data Buoy Office		www.ndbc.gov
NOAA Coastal Services Center		www.csc.noaa.gov
NOAA Watch (hazards)		www.noaawatch.gov
NOAA Weather Radio		www.nws.noaa.gov/nwr

Electric Shock Drowning

People die each year in the U.S. while swimming in freshwater around boats berthed at piers that supply AC shore power. Electric Shock Drowning (ESD) is called the invisible killer and there needs to be more publicity and boater education about this deadly process.

Any wise person would not step into a swimming pool if he/she saw an energized electrical cord submerged in the water. We all know better. Why then, are people so comfortable entering the water around boats in a marina? They too have the potential to kill swimmers by transmission of AC voltage and current from metal components on the boat's submerged hull.

Here are some basic facts that all boaters should know:

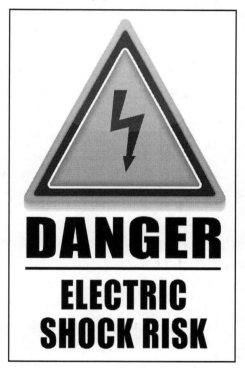

- Saltwater is 500 times more conductive than freshwater and stray electrical current can easily find a ground for dissipation. However, when AC current is discharged into freshwater, a nearby swimmer's body becomes the equivalent of a sponge for the stray electrical charge.

- Stray DC current from boats does not kill swimmers.

- Small boats typically have 30-Amp AC service from a shore power source but only 0.1 Amp discharged from a boat or submerged power cord then into a nearby swimmer is lethal. This is equal to one-third of the current needed to illuminate a standard 40-watt light bulb.

- ESD is normally caused by an electrical fault or grounding problem in a shore power cable or aboard the vessel. A trained boater will easily be able to detect these problems.

- Marina personnel should conduct annual checks for electrical faults around their piers but boaters should have a trained marine electrician conduct tests if a problem is suspected.

- All marinas prohibit swimming within 100 yards of docks to prevent ESD and potential accidents with moving vessels.

- If you're swimming and feel tingling or electrical shocks, shout to other people about your problem and get out of the water, preferably far from boats and the pier that provides AC power. Don't encourage them to jump in to save you.

- If you witness a person experiencing ESD, do not enter the water, get them out some other way and have the AC power shut off at its source.

- ESD victims often respond to Cardiopulmonary Resuscitation (CPR) so administer this life saving procedure as soon as possible on dry land.

- For prevention of ESD casualties, do not let swimmers come within 100 yards of a boat or pier that has active AC shore power.

From a common sense standpoint, if you notice that your vessel's propellers, rudders and shafts are heavily pitted and/or your zinc anodes are dissolving quicker than normal, it is likely your vessel has a serious electrical problem. Have it checked by an experienced marine electrician.

An excellent article titled "ESD Explained - What every boater needs to know about Electric Shock Drowning" by B. Leonard was published by Boat US (see article at www.boatus.com for July 2013).

Mr. Kevin Ritz, who lost a son to ESD, is a strong advocate for ESD prevention and education. His article "Electric Shock Drowning: The Invisible Killer" has been published by the American Boat & Yacht Council (2012) and a video of his compelling presentation can be viewed online.

> ### • AUTHOR RECOMMENDATION •
>
> *All boaters should read the above articles and educate others about ESD. Whenever boating in freshwater and docking at piers with AC shore power, consider the water is 'hot' from stray electrical current until you have proven otherwise. Freshwater conditions conducive to ESD are found in lakes and rivers, but do not overlook riverine areas, estuaries and marinas where freshwater may reside above saltwater which occurs naturally due to density differences in such locations.*

Statistics on Boating Deaths

The U.S. Coast Guard report on 2013 annual statistics of recreational vessels provides an extensive analysis of boating related accidents and deaths, based upon accident reports filed (a federal mandate). Some of the key findings are shown below:

2013 Boating Related Deaths			
Total boating related deaths	Number of vessels	Fatality rate (national)	Fatalities by lightning (national)
560	12,013,496 registered recreational	4.7 deaths per 1,000 vessels – PER YEAR!	0.0001 deaths per 1,000 persons - PER YEAR (33 in 318,000,000 persons)

Conclusion: Boating fatalities were 45,291 times more likely than death by lightning.

Boating fatalities by highest number incurred in each state		
State	Deaths	Deaths per 1,000 vessels
Florida	58	6.7
California	37	4.5
Texas	31	5.4
Michigan	21	2.6
New York	18	3.9

Conclusion: States with the highest boating fatalities contained the largest number of large vessels. One may suppose that small boats are more safe but statistics below do not support that premise.

Boating fatalities by age			
Age of deceased	Deaths	Age of vessel operator	Deaths
< 19 yrs	49	< 25 yrs	63
20 – 39	174	26 - 35	80
40 – 59	206	36 – 55	214
> 60	124	> 55	168

Conclusions: The middle-aged category of boaters suffered the most fatalities. Additionally, the most boating deaths occurred while middle-age persons were the vessel operators.

Vessel type involved in boating fatalities		
Type of vessel	Deaths	Percentage
Open motor boat	272	48.6%
Cabin motor vessel	25	4.5%
Sail boat	13	2.3%
Houseboat	2	0.5%
Other (including small boats and Personal Water Craft)	267	47.7%
TOTAL	560 total	

Conclusion: 96 percent of boating fatalities occurred in open motor boats or small craft.

Vessel length involved in boating fatalities	
Vessel length (ft)	**Deaths (including drowning)**
<16	264
16 – 25	219
26 – 39	30
40 – 64	5
> 65	7

Conclusion: The vast majority of boating fatalities occurred in boats less than 26 feet long.

Primary factor contributing to 2013 boating deaths	
Operation of vessel	**Deaths**
Alcohol use	75
Operator inattention	57
Operator inexperience	34
Excessive speed	19
Improper lookout	18
Navigation rules violation	15
Electric Shock Drowning	0*

Conclusions: Alcohol consumption while boating was the leading cause of death.

* Apparently, not a single death was caused by ESD in 2013.

General location of boating fatalities in 2013	
Water body	**Deaths**
Lakes	265
Rivers	169
Bays, Harbors & Marinas	74
Ocean & Gulf of Mexico	40
Great Lakes	12

Conclusion: The majority of boating fatalities occurred in freshwater and close to shore.

· CHAPTER 12 ·
Scheduling and Rates

Reservations

The procedure for reserving a slip for your vessel differs widely among marinas. All desirable marinas have a waiting list that is updated frequently by marina management personnel. In some geographic areas, marina operations are restricted to specific seasons, causing intense competition at these locations because of the limited time for boating. Boaters who live in such areas must familiarize themselves with the dates these marinas open and close. Even more important is the date when the annual waiting list begins to accept applicants, as some lists start fresh each year.

Examples of reservation procedures at various marina types are given below:

- Municipal marinas in small towns often have tremendous demand for their relatively few slips. Consequently the marina manger or harbormaster often requires applicants to prove residency in the town/city as the first step to get on the waiting list. The applicant that's first on the list must wait until an existing tenant gives up or forfeits his/her slip and this occurs rarely. I know of a small town in Massachusetts where being tenth on the list meant that you may not get a slip for at least a decade. For this reason, dry-dock marinas have been sprouting up adjacent to many of the busy 'wet' marinas and harbors.

- Marinas in larger municipalities typically have larger marinas and waiting lists that are often shorter and quicker. Typically the list is maintained objectively and posted publicly so applicants can't accuse anyone of favoritism.

- Private yacht clubs are often the most difficult marinas to obtain a slip because of the restrictive membership process, substantial joining fee and considerable waiting lists at some facilities.

- Private, multi-use marinas also manage reservations by a waiting list but the procedure for assigning slips can be subjective at some facilities, as discussed in Chapter 2 with regard to applicants needing to be cooperative during the process. Otherwise, an applicant may never get to the top of the list.

- For Dockominiums (Equity Slips) typically "money talks" and there often are slips available if the applicant can meet the financial requirements.

Slip Rates and Duration

Before discussing marina rates, it is important to remind boaters that significant discounts can sometimes be negotiated (in advance) if the owner is a member of Boat U.S., Active Captain or other marine organizations. Certainly inquire about all discount programs offered by the marina.

At most facilities, slips can be leased for various time durations that range from one day to multiple years. To begin this discussion it's necessary to first illustrate the two most common methods for calculating rates:

1. The simplest rate structure is quoted according to "length overall" of the vessel, measured from the tip of the pulpit or bowsprit to the aft-most part of the boat (e.g., swim step). This method is especially necessary when leasing long or side-tie piers where slip lengths are not predetermined.

2. The other rate type is quoted according to the specific length of a slip, regardless of the vessel length. For example, if a vessel is 35 feet long and the marina has only 30- and 40-foot slips, the boater would have to pay for the 40-foot slip although his/her vessel is considerably shorter. Vessels are not assigned slips in which the vessel would be considerably longer than the slip length. Some marinas do not allow any over-hang.

In terms of dollars, slip rates are normally quoted according to lease duration as shown below, regardless of whether the calculation is based upon method 1 or 2 above:

R(day) = $X per foot per day

R (month) = $XX per foot per month

or, for lease of a 40-foot slip (method 2) or berthing of a 40-foot vessel (method 1), rates can be quoted simply as:

$$W = \underline{\$XXXX \text{ per month}}$$

Note that Transient day rates often range from $2/ft to over $6/ft depending upon the facility, timing and occupancy level. Monthly rates are normally much lower than Transient (day) rates. It follows that Seasonal and Annual rates are quoted lower than Monthly rates at most facilities. For example, rates are given below for a 40-foot vessel at a high-end marina in a tourist area:

Example Rate Chart		
Rate	Cost	Total Cost
Transient day rate	$5 per foot per day	$200
Monthly rate	$30 per foot per month	$1,200 (one-fifth of Transient rate)
Annual rate	$15 per foot per month	$7,200 (half of Monthly rate)

Most facilities have a small number of transient slips available for vessels that wish to stay for only a few nights. Marinas make a high profit when leasing transient slips but longer-term leases generate the majority of the revenue at most marinas.

Other Fee Considerations

When boaters obtain price quotations from marinas, it is essential they understand the charges included in the overall monthly or annual fee. Here's an example of a worst-case scenario:

A boater is ecstatic he can lease a slip in the marina of his choice, as confirmed by a phone call from the marina office. The rate he had been quoted was $1,200 per month ($30 per foot per month) for the 40-foot slip that was available — ideal for his 35-foot vessel. Although this was considerably more than the $910 per month he had been quoted at his second-choice marina, he really liked the pool and marina restaurant at his first choice. The $910 (tax included) had been calculated from $26 per foot per month times 35 feet because marina 'B' only charged by actual vessel length, rather than by the length of the slip.

Although marina 'A' was a few hundred dollars more expensive than his second choice, he committed to leasing the slip over the phone because he was told the next person on the waiting list would take the slip if he didn't commit right then. "Okay sign me up" said the happy boater.

When he arrived at marina 'A' he was happy to quickly sign the marina tenant agreement then sign the form for automatic bank withdrawal for his monthly slip rental. His jaw dropped when he saw a total of $1,445 per month. "What's this about?" he said to the marina finance person with a big frown.

"The breakdown is like this: $1,200 per month for the slip, $150 for the resort fee, and $95 for state tax, which totals $1,445. And that does not include your monthly electric bill that will be metered and based upon actual usage. For your size boat, electrical costs typically range from $75 per month to $150 depending on how much you use your air conditioning. You chose not to be live-aboard which could have added another $125 per month, plus tax, for one person only."

Realistically, the boater can expect a bill of around $1,550 per month including an average electric bill. At marina 'B' he would have been paying $910 per month for the slip (tax included) plus their flat fee of $50 for electrical; no other charges. Thus, marina 'A' ended up costing him 61 percent more than marina 'B'. Had he taken time to assess all the costs at marina 'A', he might have decided that the nice pool and restaurant were not worth the additional $590 per month.

· CHAPTER 13 ·
Marina Tenant Agreements

Marina contracts for boaters normally consist of three parts: 1) Financial Contract, 2) marina tenant agreement with legal terms and insurance requirements, and 3) rules and regulations which are more detailed and informal. Three important issues you must consider before signing a marina contract are identified below:

- Marinas always require the applicant to demonstrate existing insurance on the vessel, including protection and indemnity coverage, typically to a limit of $500,000 or $1,000,000. Check the value of your P&I coverage. If it's too low, any delay in increasing your coverage could cause you to lose your intended slip at the new marina.

- For vessels longer than 40-feet, most insurance policies require annual inspection of onboard fire prevention equipment by a certified fire safety representative. Do not let this testing lapse because any insurance claims could be negated, your insurance policy could be cancelled and your marina contract could be terminated if you cannot demonstrate active coverage.

- Marina tenant agreements typically do not state that rates are subject to change at any time but that is certainly the case, especially at private facilities. It's wise to ask marina management if they anticipate any near-term rate increases. Even if they say no, ask if they plan any major construction or facility maintenance projects, as these are likely to trigger a rate increase for tenants. Recently, some marinas have increased their rates to long-term tenants by more than 30 percent.

Rules and Regulations

All marina tenant agreements (or sometimes called Contract for Private Wharfage) are accompanied by specific rules and regulations that must be followed by tenants and guests. The rules differ considerably among marinas and also across city and state jurisdictions, likely because of official regulations. To illustrate the wide variety of marina guidelines boaters can encounter, examples of specific terms have been selected from multiple marina tenant agreements. This list certainly is not 'all inclusive'; rather, its purpose is to demonstrate diversity in terms that can be encountered. Many of these stipulations make good sense whereas others are over-restrictive and quite amusing. Below they are presented in no particular order or degree of importance.

1. Permitted Use

Berthing of vessel for recreational boating only, unless approved in writing.

Commercial use of vessel in slip or marina is prohibited without prior written approval.

2. Children

Children under 12 years of age are not permitted on docks without parental supervision.

Non-swimmers and toddlers shall wear life jackets while on docks or vessel decks.

3. Restricted Access Through Marina Gates

For purposes of safety, security and privacy, owners and guests are prohibited from opening gates for any individual not personally known to be a marina tenant.

4. Projections Beyond End of Berth

No vessel or part of vessel can extend more than 3 feet beyond the end of the berth into the waterway unless authorized in writing. Similarly, nothing must extend forward over the main head dock.

5. Live-Aboard Definition

A vessel that is inhabited for five consecutive days or total of 10 days within a 30-day period.

6. Small Boat Storage

For slips less than 40 feet in length, all dinghies, kayaks and water toys must be stored aboard the vessel.

In larger slips, one water craft may be stored in the slip provided that it does not extend beyond the confines of the slip.

7. Noise and Conduct

No disturbing noises are permitted on docks or anywhere in the marina, especially between hours of 10 p.m. and 7 a.m. Conduct must be reasonable at all times.

Parties are not permitted on docks without prior marina permission.

8. Engine Operation

Engines cannot be operated while in gear while vessel is secured to dock.

Engines shall not be run for more than 15 minutes while in slip.

Vessels are not permitted to run engines or noise-making equipment between hours of 5 p.m. and 9 a.m. except in emergencies or while vessel is leaving or entering slip.

9. Vessel Speed within Marina

Vessel speed limit in marina waters is specified as "steerage only". No speeds greater than 5 mph or vessel wakes are permitted.

10. Improper Vessel Handling

If dockmaster deems vessel is being handled improperly or in an unsafe manner, owner's vessel will be prohibited from the marina.

11. Vessel Registration

Vessel must possess current state and/or federal registration.

12. Compliance with State and Local Regulations

Owner is subject to restrictions imposed by government authorities.

Owner is responsible for actions and behavior of owner's associates, including guests and any subcontracted labor.

13. Vessel Condition and Inspections

Owner must maintain vessel in good operational condition. Vessel must be able to move under its own propulsion.

Marina reserves the right to inspect vessel to determine if properly identified and equipped for safe operation in accordance with U.S. Coast Guard and local regulations.

14. Use of Slip Only by Designated Vessel

Owner may not authorize or sublease other vessels to occupy slip during absence of the primary vessel specified under contract.

15. Approval of Equipment used for Vessel Dockage

All equipment used to secure and prevent damage to docked vessel must be approved by marina.

16. Maintenance of Slip and Marina

Owner shall maintain slip and adjacent docks in good condition; no alterations.

17. Disposal of Refuse

Owner shall not dispose into marina waste container, any flammable or hazardous liquids, batteries, vessel parts or the like.

No item weighing more than 20 pounds shall be disposed.

18. Storage of Owner's Items on Docks

Owner may store items in a single, while fiberglass dock box adjacent to the owner's vessel.

Bicycles must be stored aboard vessel and not on docks. Bicycles may also be stored in bicycle racks provided by the marina.

19. Dock Steps

Temporary steps for boarding vessel are permitted on dock but shall not be wider than half the width of the dock and no more than 3 feet in length. Marina may prohibit steps that are visually offensive.

20. Indemnification of Marina

Owner indemnifies marina for owner or vessel damages incurred on property or vessel.

21. Relocation of Slip

Marina may change slip assignment of owner's vessel.

22. Marina Rights for Temporary Movement of Vessel

Marina may require owner to temporarily move vessel to another slip while construction work is being conducted by marina.

Similarly, marina may require vessel movement during boat shows, holiday events or parade functions.

23. Marina Actions on Owner's Vessel

Owner will reimburse marina for any costs incurred while marina relocates vessel or conducts actions to prevent vessel damage while owner is absent.

Marina is held harmless of any damages or costs incurred as a result of voluntary actions.

24. Compliance with Sanitation Regulations

Vessel must have sanitary equipment that meets regulations and complies with discharge prohibitions.

25. Value of Owner's Protection and Indemnity Insurance

Owner shall demonstrate existing P&I insurance to specified limit. In some states, environmental liability insurance must be also demonstrated to cover any damages resulting from hazardous releases from the vessel.

26. Owner's Liability for Damage to Environment

Owner shall not release wastes or hazardous substances into the water. Owner is responsible for all clean-up expenses.

Owner shall reimburse marina for any costs incurred to remedy environmental problems caused by owner or owner's vessel.

27. Owner's Liability for Damage to Marina

Owner shall reimburse marina for any damage and costs incurred to remedy damage to marina caused by owner or owner's vessel.

28. Property Damage Caused by Irresistible Forces

Marina shall not be liable for personal injury or property damage/loss caused by fire, storm, theft, winds, acts of God or any other irresistible force.

29. Posting of Signs

No signage can be displayed on vessel for commercial purposes without prior written approval. This includes For Sale signs.

30. Repairs

Major repairs such as typically conducted in a boatyard are not permitted aboard, at, or near vessel or marina.

31. Outside Contractors

Contractors hired by owner to work on vessel must be approved in advance by marina and demonstrate adequate liability insurance.

Contractors must sign in at the marina office prior to work each day and sign out upon completion of the day's work.

32. Hazardous Spills from Vessel

If a leak or spill of any fuel or other combustible liquid occurs within the interior of the vessel, owner shall immediately contact marina and local fire department to report such leak or spill. Owner shall contact an emergency towing service to have vessel removed from the marina until problem is remedied.

33. Extended Vessel Absence from Marina

Owner shall notify marina of plans for an extended cruise, typically more than one week in duration marina has right to rent vacant slip to transient boater with no financial gain for owner.

34. Electrical Service

Marina does not guarantee quality or continuity of electrical power on piers. Marina reserves right to interrupt utilities during repair, construction or renovation to marina. Owner accepts all liability associated with use of owner's power cords.

35. Water, Power and Cable Lines

Such connections shall not be run across main docks nor be affixed to dock.

36. Dock Carts

Dock carts are provided for use by tenants and their guests. Dock carts must be cleaned and returned to the marina storage area after each use.

37. Use of Swimming Pool, Spa and Fitness Area

Owner and up to five guests may use the marina facilities during the times posted for use. Paid vessel crew members and captains are not permitted to use marina recreational facilities.

38. Television Antennae and Satellite Dishes

No external television antennae are permitted aboard vessels. No satellite dishes may be affixed to pilings or other marina property without written approval.

39. Hazardous Activities and Barbecues

Handling fuel on docks is strictly prohibited. Barbecues and similar fire hazards are prohibited on docks. Charcoal barbecues are also prohibited aboard vessels. Propane barbecues are permitted on vessels only.

40. Controlling Depths

Marina is not responsible for water depth in marina slips or channels.

Marina is held harmless for any damages that may occur to owner's vessel due to shoaling.

41. Security Service

Marina may provide security service on the facility but is by courtesy. Marina is not responsible for any loss or damage to owner's property by breach of security.

42. Solicitations

Unauthorized persons are prohibited from soliciting business or offering goods for sale on premises of the marina.

43. Severe Storms

Marina requires all vessels to leave the waterway basin during major storms. If a vessel is granted permission to remain in the marina, owner is liable for costs and damages to other vessels and marina property.

Adequate liability insurance must be demonstrated by the owner.

44. Laundry Restrictions

Laundering can only be performed in the interior of the vessel. No drying of laundry items can be conducted outside or in vessel's rigging.

45. Fishing and Fish Cleaning

Fishing is prohibited from vessels and Marina facilities. No fish cleaning is permitted on the docks or in slips

46. Pets Policy

Owner's pets must be under control at all times and picked up after.

Cats must be carried to and from the vessel and at no time be free to run on docks. Dogs must be leashed or carried in a container when not in vessels. Other than birds, pets may not be left unattended on vessels.

· CHAPTER 14 ·
Buying and Selling a Yacht

Boaters typically own more than one vessel in their lifetime. As previously referenced, the Marinas.com Member Survey of 2015 indicates that 62 percent of the respondents have owned two or more boats. Another 28 percent have owned a single boat and it's likely that these individuals are not close to buying the farm; consequently it's probable they will purchase one or more additional boats in their lifetime.

Many boaters upgrade to a newer and/or larger vessel every few years, much like car owners, but land vehicles are a necessity for most people whereas recreational vessels are often toys or luxuries of a floating sort. A fair percentage of boaters choose their last vessel for a retirement home although its size is often prohibitive for family reunions.

To sum it up, everyone who owns a substantial-sized vessel (say 30 feet or larger) will someday be selling his/her craft and will consider engaging a yacht broker. Owners of small boats often attempt sale-by-owner rather than pay a broker's commission and this is becoming the norm for small-boat sales with numerous boat sale websites emerging every year. For larger boats however, the complexity of the sale increases greatly with the need to engage marine surveyors, conduct sea trials, certified engine and fuel tests, perform haul-out inspections, etc. All of these necessities make the process of vessel sale more challenging for the owner/seller.

If you may be within a year or two selling your vessel, begin now to search for an experienced, licensed, reputable, cooperative and trustworthy yacht broker who has a proven record of selling your type of vessel. If you own a motor vessel, don't choose a broker who mainly sells sailing yachts; and vice versa. Wise buyers often seek out individual brokers and yacht sales firms who specialize in the type of vessel they want to purchase. You want your broker to be prominent to this buyer.

If you're buying and have a good broker representing you in that specific market, they'll likely know many vessels that fall within the general category you favor, thereby saving you considerable time and possibly money, if you can negotiate with two separate sellers of the same type of vessel. Often with boats, it's a buyer's market because many boat owners need to sell for desperate reasons – sad but perfect for the buyer.

Whether you are considering selling, buying or both, a good first step is to go online and search for boats in your general category. This is helpful for sellers because you can see sale (asking) prices for comparable vessels in addition to how long they've been on the market. Buyers can quickly search for a specific boat manufacturer and model, check the sales inventory then determine whether prices for a specific vessel vary with geography (e.g., either between states, or East Coast versus West Coast). All of this initial research can be done before engaging your Broker.

One of the best websites in the U.S. for yacht shopping (both new and pre-owned) is Yachtworld.com. This free website is excellent for searches by prospective buyers but realize that all of these vessels can only by purchased through brokers (who paid a considerable sum to post their boat listing).

Recommendations for Sellers

- Go to Yachtworld.com and conduct an advanced search for vessels of the same general configuration/model, manufacturer and year.

- Assess vessel prices and see how they differ by the year of manufacture; make a simple graph on paper (or your PC) with sale price on the y-axis and year on the x-axis to determine a general depreciation rate (slope of the line through the most points on the graph) for your vessel type.

- Select a good sale price for your vessel using the depreciation line — higher than the line if your vessel is in excellent condition and has many additional features than the standard model; lower if your vessel isn't in Bristol condition.

- Consult with your broker to decide on the initial sale price then have him/her post the listing.

- Recognize that it's likely you will have to lower the listed price a few times before the sale, then again during the final negotiations.

- If there have been no interested parties or offers during the first two months the vessel has been advertised, consider dropping the price 5 percent.

- Continue to lower the price every couple months, even if only a small amount, to keep your vessel's listing active.

Recommendations for Buyers

- Again go to Yachtworld.com and conduct an advanced search for vessels that meet your general search guidelines.

- Assess whether there is sufficient inventory of appealing vessels for sale in your geographic area or whether you should expand your search region.

- Select a group of vessels to view and have your Broker make appointments.

- Never visit a for sale vessel without your broker or he/she will not gain part of the commission on the purchase. Note that sellers' brokers are typically unwilling to reduce their commission even when a buyer's broker is not involved, so there is no gain for the buyer to exclude his/her own broker.

- When you have found a good vessel, have the broker speak 'off line' with the selling broker (without you there) in an attempt to learn about seller motivation, how long the vessel has been on the market, whether there are other interested buyers, etc.

- Trust only your (buyer's) broker, as he/she is looking out for your best interests, typically not the role of a seller's broker who will repeatedly tell you how wonderful the boat is.

- Make a relatively low first offer but don't anger the seller with a ridiculous 'low ball' offer. Expect a few rounds of price negotiations and be respectful of the owner.

- And most important of all, never let the seller's broker select the individuals or companies to perform the hull and engine surveys for boats they are selling. This can be a major conflict of interest, often with boat problems not being identified, at the buyer's later demise.

References

Nuisance Algae References

Dutra, R. (2011). Is Red Tide Taking Over Middletown Beaches? Open On-line Post to Middletown Patch, Middletown, RI. July 13, 2011

FBAMS (2000). Rust and Rotten Eggs: Iron and Sulfur in Florida Bay. Florida Bay Watch Report. A Synthesis document of the Florida Bay Adjacent Marine Systems Science Program. August 2000

U.S. Coast Guard References

Navigation Rules and Regulations Handbook (Rules of the Road). U.S. Coast Guard. 2014

Recreational Boating Statistics - 2013. U.S. Coast Guard - Commandant Publication P16754.27. 2014

Storm Surge References

Needham, H. and B. D. Keim (2011). Storm Surge: Physical Processes and an Impact Scale, Recent Hurricane Research - Climate, Dynamics, and Societal Impacts, Prof. Anthony Lupo (Ed.), ISBN: 978-953-307-238-8, InTech. Available from: http://www.intechopen.com/books/recent-hurricane-research-climate-dynamicsand-societal-impacts/storm-surge-physical-processes-and-an-impact-scale

Resio, D.T. and J.J. Westerink (2008). Modeling the Physics of Storm Surge. Physics Today. September 2008. pp 33-38.

Rhome J. (2013). Forecasting and Modeling Storm Surge. Presentation at NOAA Hurricane Center (hurricanes.gov/surge). Access via: http://www.nhc.noaa.gov/ outreach/presentations/2013_08nhcL311_stormSurgeForecastingProducts.pdf

Tsunami Reference

Dunbar, P.K. and C. S. Weaver (2008). National Tsunami Hazard Assessment: Historical Record and Sources for Waves. Prepared for the National Tsunami Hazard Mitigation Program.

Meteo-tsunami References

Bailey, K., C. DiVeglio and A. Welty (2014). An Examination of the June 2013 East Coast Meteotsunami Captured By NOAA Observing Systems. NOAA Technical Report NOS CO-OPS 079

Fraser, D. (2013). Weather Creates Rare Cape Cod Tsunami. Cape Cod Times. June 15, 2013

Lightning References

Boat US (2010). Lightning! Flash, BANG! Your Boat's Been Hit – Now What. Published August 2010

Curran, E.B., R.L. Holle and R.E. López (2000). Lightning casualties and damages in the United States from 1959 to 1994. Journal of Climate, 13, 3448-3453.

Holle, R.L., R.E. Lopez and E.B. Curran (1999). Distributions of Lightning-Caused Casualties and Damages Since 1959 in the United States. Presented at 11th Conference on Applied Climatology, American Meteorological Society. January 1999

Holle, R. (2013). Lightning fatalities by State 1959 – 2012. Vaisala report

Electric Shock Drowning References

Leonard, B. (2013). ESD Explained - What every boater needs to know about Electric Shock Drowning. Boat US. July 2013

Ritz, K. (2012). Electric Shock Drowning: The Invisible Killer. American Boat & Yacht Council

Glossary

Abiki – The Japanese word for meteo-tsunami

Ablative bottom paints – A type of anti-fouling bottom paint that is characterized as a 'soft coat' which acts similar to time-released medication that gradually releases a bit of the biocide compound. These paints (also called sloughing paints) often have to be replaced more frequently than 'hard coat' bottom paints that bottom cleaners erode less easily.

AC – Alternating current, typically 115 or 230 volts

Acoustic transducer – An electro-mechanical device mounted on the bottom of a vessel for acoustic measurement of water depth.

Anoxic – The term used for water that has essentially been depleted of dissolved oxygen.

Anti-fouling – A broad category of chemical coatings (paints) used on the bottom of vessels to prevent the growth of biofouling organisms.

Aquaculture – Controlled farming of fish and shellfish in fresh or salt-water environments. Pens (restrictive netting) are used to raise fish; baskets and vertical strings are used for raising shellfish.

At-sea discharge – The act of pumping bilge water or waste water (e.g., sewage) from a vessel, the latter being permitted only greater than three nautical miles offshore the U.S. coastline.

Bait fish – The term used to describe a broad variety of small fish that are eventually used as bait for fishing.

Berthing – Docking a vessel in a slip or pier of a marina.

Best Management Practices – A formal document or protocol outlining optimum procedures for a specific business or activity.

Bilge – The lowest interior compartment of a vessel's hull, often with multiple compartments that are intended to contain liquid or gaseous wastes.

Biocide – A chemical mixture used to kill or retard growth of nuisance organisms

Biofouling – Growth of nuisance organisms (marine plants and animals) on the bottom of a vessel.

Black water – Waste water aboard a vessel that is collected from onboard toilets.

Boat ramp – On land, an inclined roadway upon which motor vehicles are backed down to launch small boats. Typically a trailered boat is launched when the trailer is backed down and partially submerged so the boat floats off.

Boatyard – An area on land used for storage and maintenance of vessels of all sizes.

Bonding system – Interconnection of metal components within a vessel for the purpose of electrical isolation and reduced galvanic corrosion which can occur when un-bonded metal components are submerged in seawater.

Bottom cleaning – The process of removing nuisance marine growth from the bottom of a vessel, often conducted by divers while the vessel's hull is submerged but also by power wash spraying when the hull is out of the water.

Bought the Farm – A mariner's expression used to describe when another mariner ends his sailing career by moving onshore for the last time, not necessarily because of death but the end result is nearly as bad.

Bowsprit – A pole or beam that extends forward of a vessel's bow or stem, typically on sailboats for attaching stays for the jib or foresail.

Brackish – Water that is a mixture of fresh water and seawater, thus characterized by moderate salinity. Water clarity is independent of brackish characteristics.

Bristol – The term used to describe the condition of a vessel when it is better than factory new and loaded with extra features.

Cable Master system – A commercial product designed to automatically coil a shore power cable into a sealed cylindrical container below deck, by means of an electric motor.

Cast net – A flat, circular mesh net with weights on its periphery that is thrown by hand to catch small fish at or near the water's surface.

Catamaran – A power or sailing vessel that has two parallel hulls (pontoons) for distributed buoyancy and which are connected rigidly between. A tri-marine is similar but with three partially submerged, parallel hulls.

Center-console boat – A relatively small (typically 18- to 30-foot) open boat that has a central pedestal for steering and control of motors.

Charm School – An old expression for a hypothetical place where rude and obstinate persons are sent to learn better behavior, manners and cooperation.

Charter boat – A fishing boat equipped with Captain and crew that can be hired (chartered) for offshore fishing, typically by up to six paying customers for whole or half-day trips.

Chase boat – A boat whose purpose is to accompany a relatively larger vessel and transport crew and supplies to/from shore. Medium size vessels have dinghies whereas very large vessels and mega-yachts have chase boats that can range in size from 30 to 75 feet in length, often towed or cruising independently near the larger vessel between ports of call.

Clean Marina Program – A voluntary program established in many U.S. States for marinas to better control their adverse effects on the environment.

City water – Fresh water that is supplied to marina docks from municipal water systems, as for land-based properties.

Cockpit – The rear deck of a vessel that is not enclosed.

Confused sea – Surface waves that are irregular in height and direction of propagation, typically caused by interaction of waves from multiple sources and directions (e.g., wind waves, swell and vessel wakes).

Control depth – The depth of a channel or water body, typically described as the least depth that is guaranteed by recent dredging operations.

Cutlass bearing – A circular, annular bearing through which a vessel's engine shaft extends as it passes from the inner engine compartment to the exterior water.

DC – Direct current as is provided by batteries.

Dark N' Stormy – A popular alcoholic drink of mariners, concocted from Gosling's Rum, ginger beer and cuttings from a fresh lime, served or ice. Thirst quenching, even in heavy weather.

Davit – A J-shaped device used to lift equipment small boats aboard a larger vessel. A vertical post is attached to a near-horizontal beam to facilitate the lifting arm. Pulleys and line or strong wire are used for hoisting, typically with a winch or a hand crank.

Derecho – A long (greater than 200-mile) line of severe thunderstorms and high winds that move rapidly across landmasses.

Derelict boat – Any type or size of boat in serious disrepair, often unattended.

Dinghy – A very small (typically less than 15-ft) boat used to transport people and supplies to a larger vessel. Dinghies are made of various materials (e.g., wood, aluminum, fiberglass and inflatable pontoons, some with rigid bottoms) and can be either motor powered or propelled by rowing.

Diurnal tide – One type of astronomical tide that results in only one high water and one low water event per day.

Dock – Any type of structure that allows direct access from shore to a water body. It must be attached to land but can be either fixed or floating.

Dock box – A watertight box used to store boating paraphernalia. Typically white and constructed of fiberglass, dock boxes can be securely mounted on a dock or aboard a vessel.

Dock Boy – A male or female employee of the marina whose primary role is to assist boaters while berthing their vessel. Assistance can also be provided during fueling, taking on freshwater or transporting supplies onboard.

Dock cart – A small, un-motorized cart with wheels that is used to transport supplies to berthed vessels.

Dockmaster – The person in charge of physical operations and vessels within a marina.

Dockominium – Equivalent to an Equity Slip Ownership, a facility that allows vessel owners to purchase a slip for permanent or very long-term ownership, as for condominiums on land.

Double-slip – Within a marina, a wide U-shaped configuration that allow two vessels to be berthed side-by-side with no pier between their parallel hulls.

Dredging – The mechanical means of removing bottom sediment to make a water body deeper.

Dry-dock marina – A facility that offers on-land storage to vessels, either on racks within large storage buildings or in uncovered parking lots. Dry-dock marinas do not necessarily have to be waterside, as trailered boats can be transported to the dry-dock marina for storage. Waterside facilities allow easy loading but most do not have in-water slips for dockage.

Dry storage – Any type of boat storage (trailered, racked, blocked, etc.) where the vessel is not in the water.

Electric Shock Drowning – (ESD) Electrocution caused by AC current that enters fresh water where a person is swimming. The source of the current may be from a poorly grounded vessel, a shore power cord or a submerged electrical motor.

Embayment – A concave area of coastline that is partially sheltered from waves but whose water readily exchanges with the adjacent sea.

End-tie slip – The part of a main dock that is farthest from shore and accommodates vessels tied perpendicular to the direction of the main dock. Similarly, smaller piers can have end-tie slips also. T-docks is the common name for docks that have end-tie slips.

Equity Slip Ownership – Vessel slips that are sold rather than leased. Some facilities have more complex equity ownership arrangements.

Fairway – The narrow waterway between adjacent piers of a marina.

Fendering – Placement of fenders or flexible buoys between a vessel and its adjacent pier to prevent chaffing damage to the vessel's hull.

Fetch – The distance over which wind blows during generation of local surface waves.

Finger pier – A small pier that is typically attached perpendicular to a main dock. Piers often delineate the boundaries of a vessel slip.

Fishing grounds – A geographic region known for good fishing.

Fixed dock – A shore-side physical structure that remains stationary and independent of variations in the local water level.

Floating dock – A shore-side physical structure whose top, horizontal surface remains at the same height above the water level regardless of vertical fluctuations in water level. Floating docks must be loosely attached to fixed docks, pilings or shore structures to prevent horizontal escape.

Flushing – The physical process of horizontal water movement into or out of a confined region.

Flying Bridge – The upper helm of a sportfishing boat or motor vessel that is typically open to the weather.

Fuel polishing system – Various types of systems designed to clean vessel fuel of particulate matter, water or other liquids that have different specific gravities than the fuel when pure.

Galvanic corrosion – With regard to vessels in the marine environment, galvanic corrosion is the dissolution of metals (often called marine corrosion or electrolysis) caused when dissimilar metals are in electrical contact with each other while immersed in seawater, an effective electrolytic solution. Galvanic corrosion can also can be initiated by other nearby sources of stray electrical current.

Gangway – A ramp used by passengers to access a vessel.

Gosling's – Quality dark rum distilled in Bermuda. The essential ingredient of the Dark N' Stormy cocktail of many mariners.

Gray water – Waste water generated by sinks, showers, dishwashers and other cleaning activities aboard vessels. In some regions, clean bilge water is considered gray water. Wastes from toilets are not to be included in gray water.

Green flash – A visual phenomenon that is sometimes observed as the sun sets on the horizon on clear evenings, or similarly at sunrise. A flash of green light occurs above the upper rim of the sun for one or two seconds when atmospheric conditions are optimum, causing the sunlight to separate into different colors of the spectrum.

Green materials – Products that are composed of renewable resources.

Ground tackle – Submerged components of a mooring system including the anchor and a length of chain that leads toward the surface, sometimes connecting to line.

Gunnel – The edge or horizontal surface on top of the outer, vertical wall of a vessel's hull such as surrounding a cockpit.

Handline – A small diameter fishing line that is used without a rod or reel. Before synthetic lines were created, natural fibers were used for fishing line and a tar coating was applied to prevent rotting.

Harbormaster – The person in charge of all operations within a harbor, including marine operations, safety, piers, parking and other facilities.

Harbor of Refuge – A port, inlet or other body of water sheltered from heavy seas by land and in which a vessel can navigate safely and moor. The suitability of a location as a harbor of safe refuge varies for each vessel, dependent on the vessel's size, maneuverability and mooring gear.

Harmful algal bloom – When marine algae flourishes due to natural or manmade causes, resulting in harmful water quality conditions and risks to marine life and humans.

Haul-out – Removal of a vessel from the water. A term used typically for large vessels rather than small boats on trailers.

Head — The name for a toilet on a vessel.

Inverse-barometer effect – The natural condition by which low atmospheric (barometric) pressure will allow the sea level to rise while in contrast, high atmospheric pressure will depress sea level.

Irresistible Forces – In some marina tenant agreements, marinas are not held liable for damage to vessels when caused by Irresistible Forces, defined as: fire, storms, theft, winds and acts of God – almost everything bad.

Launch – A small boat (typically between 20 and 30 feet in length) used in support functions to a larger vessel. Dinghies and tenders are smaller than launches; Chase Boats are considerably larger than launches.

Lazarette – A storage compartment that is typically below deck in the cockpit of a vessel.

Length overall – The greatest actual length of a vessel, extending from the tip of any pulpit or bowsprit to the farthest aft part of the boat or swim platform.

Line handler – A person who assists an incoming or departing vessel by tending to lines attached to the vessel or dock. Considerable skill and training are required for efficient and safe tending of lines, especially during severe weather when high tension can be applied to the lines during vessel movement.

Live-aboard – A housing status when vessel owners and/or crew stay aboard for more than the minimum allowable days per week or month permitted by a marina tenant agreement. From a different perspective, some persons proudly claim their live-aboard status which entails full-time, year-round residence aboard their vessel.

Live-well bait tank – An onboard tank situated in or near the cockpit of a fishing vessel that is used to contain live bait in fresh seawater that is circulated through the tank. The term 'live' pertains to the bait being kept 'alive'. The term 'well' pertains to a container that holds water like a 'wishing well'.

Macerator pump – A special water pump that chops any solid wastes into small particulates while passing through the pump. It is normally used in conjunction with a holding tank for toilet wastes. The waste slurry is discharged into the sea via a through-hull port beneath the water line but only when the vessel is located in waters permissible for waste discharge according to U.S. Coast Guard regulations.

Marina – A shore-side facility where boats can be launched and/or stored for various lengths of time. Numerous other activities can be conducted at marinas as described in this guidebook.

Marina manager – An employee of the Marina Owner(s) who typically manages all business operations of the Marina. At some facilities, a separate Dock Master is employed to manage all marine operations at the facility, under direction of the marina manager.

Marina tenant agreement – A legal contract created by a Marina organization for lease of a vessel slip to a vessel Owner. The Agreement typically covers Owner use of marina facilities, vessel conditions, Rules and Regulations, plus many terms regarding insurance liability of vessel and marina.

Marine radio – Utilized aboard vessels of all sizes, marine radios are configured with a combined transmitter and receiver, operating on standard VHF frequency channels between 156.0 and 162.0 MHz Newer units offer Digital Selective Calling (DSC) capability to allow a distress signal to be sent simply by pressing a button.

Marine Sanitation Device – Guidelines for MSDs can be found on the website of the U.S. Coast Guard: www.uscg.mil/hq/cg5/cg5213/msd.asp. No person may operate any vessel having an installed toilet facility unless it is equipped with an installed and operable MSD of a type approved by the U.S. Coast Guard to meet the requirements of 33 CFR Part 159. There are three types of MSDs that can be certified by the U.S. Coast Guard: Types I and II are flow-through discharge devices that reduce fecal coliform bacteria levels and address floating solids. Type III is essentially a holding tank.

Mega-yacht – Definitions of yachts, super-yachts and mega-yachts are imprecise but the later are typically categorized as vessels longer than 150 feet whereas super-yachts are longer than 75 feet.

Meteo-tsunami – Similar to tsunamis, meteo-tsunamis generate large waves that inundate coastal regions but they are solely generated by intense atmospheric fronts that move quickly across coastal waters. The amplitude of meteo-tsunami waves and coastal run-up is governed by the atmospheric pressure changes associated with frontal passage and the speed of its horizontal movement.

Mixed tide – An astronomical tidal situation that is influenced both by the semi-diurnal and diurnal tides. Characteristics of high and low water vary greatly from day to day as well as between tides on the same day.

Mooring – The name typically used to describe a type of vessel anchoring arrangement, most commonly within in a harbor, where the vessel is loosely secured to a bottom anchor by line and chain (called ground tackle). Moorings anchors are stationary and permanent, sometimes unattended by a vessel. In contrast, conventional anchors are lowered at various locations then brought aboard for vessel cruising.

Municipal marina – A marina that is owned and operated by any type of government organization (e.g., town, city, state, etc.).

Named windstorm – A storm system, typically a major windstorm, that has been declared and named by the National Weather Service. They can be on land or at sea.

Neap tide – Periods of two to four days when the range of the astronomical tide is reduced by misalignment (perpendicular orientation) of the moon and sun, causing a reduction of the normal gravitational pull. Neap tides occur every two weeks but vary in amplitude throughout the year.

Non-indigenous species – A type of marine species (e.g., mussel) that has: 1) been transported from its native region by human intervention and 2) reestablished an active community of organisms in a different marine area. Depending upon the species of marine mussels, such relocation can result in major nuisance infestations or become profitable aquaculture operations.

Nor'easter – An intense low-pressure storm that intensifies off the coast of New England and drives strong on-shore winds from the northeast direction.

Nuisance algae – Excessive density of microscopic marine plants (phytoplankton) typically caused by excess nutrients. The nuisance can be the odor of decaying plant matter and/or the depletion of dissolved oxygen in the water which further causes plant and fish mortality.

Oily waste – Liquid waste from vessels, including waste oil, engine coolant and bilge water which often contains oil and coolant solutions.

On the Hard – The term used by seasoned boaters to indicate storage of a vessel on-land, typically in a paved, outdoor storage area.

Open water – A mariner's term for the area offshore of a harbor or bay where winds and seas are minimally affected by land or coastal physiography.

Overboard discharge – Disposal (typically via pumping) of liquid wastes from a vessel, including either clean water, gray water or black water.

Personal Water Craft – (PWC) See also definition of Toys. Various floating sporting devices that can be propelled by motors or human power. Examples include: jet skis, kayaks, canoes, paddleboards, sailboards, etc.

Physical Oceanographer – A marine scientist specializing in physical processes of the ocean, including waves, currents and ocean dynamics.

Physiography – Regional geomorphology including the coastal geography and topography.

Phytoplankton – Microscopic natural plants that live in the marine environment.

Pier – In the context of this marina guidebook, pier is the name for the physical structure used to secure a floating vessel within a marina. Piers also are walkways for vessel passengers and transport of supplies to vessels. Piers can be fixed or floating, in saltwater or fresh and defined synonymously with the term dock.

Piling – A stationary, vertical post of wood, concrete or steel construction used to secure boats in a marina or harbor. 'Sheet piling' is configured as a vertical wall, typically of steel, used as a retaining barrier to prevent land from caving into a harbor or marina water.

Pulpit – A raised platform that extends forward from the bow of a boat. On old fishing vessels, men would stand on the pulpit to toss a harpoon when whaling.

Pump-out – Removal of liquid sewage from a below-deck waste tank within a vessel.

Pumping station – A sewage pump-out station located on a pier or shore-side facility. They can be privately maintained or open for public use.

Purse seine – A long, vertical fishing net deployed in a circular pattern by a moving commercial fishing vessel as it wraps around a school of fish. When the ends of the vertical net are secured together, a bottom wire is pulled to close the 'purse' with the fish inside.

Rack storage – A structure designed to support a vessel while stored out of the water. Originally, racks were available for small boats in covered buildings but large racks are now more commonplace and oftentimes used outside for large vessels.

Raw water – Seawater. Preferably pumped into a vessel intentionally.

Red Tide – An excessive population of marine red algae than can become a nuisance because of it's ability to deplete local dissolved oxygen levels, resulting in fish kills and offensive odors. The patches of algae can be moved by horizontal currents but the biological problem is not caused by the tide.

Resort marina – A category of private or corporate marina facilities that are co-located with a resort hotel or condominium facility and offer excellent amenities.

Rigid Inflatable Boat – (RIB) A boat with air-filled pontoons around the sides that are permanently attached to a rigid deck/bottom make of fiberglass or aluminum. Most RIBs are less than 15 feet but some are now manufactured up to 30 feet in length.

Rissaga – The Spanish word for meteo-tsunami.

River stage – The water level measured in a river above a normal datum.

Rules of the Road – The U.S. Coast Guard's Navigation Rules and Regulations Handbook, also known as 'Rules of the Road' or

NavRules CG169, contains the International Regulations for Preventing Collisions at Sea, 1972 (72 COLREGS).

Running gear – A term used for all submerged metal propulsion (shaft, bearings and propellers) and steering (rudder) components of a vessel.

Run-up – The act of sudden inundation of a shoreline by on-shore flow of water, most typically associated with a tsunami. Its grammatical use is typically as a verb describing the movement of water and its penetration into land areas. Flooding is generally a slower process than run-up.

Rust bucket – An old mariner's term for a vessel in very poor condition, not necessarily made of steel (rusty) but definitely streaked with rust from old equipment, chain and other steel items.

Sacrificial anode – The common name for zincs that are attached to submerged metal components of vessels to reduce galvanic corrosion to more critical parts of a vessel's running gear.

Seismic sea wave – A scientifically correct name for a tsunami generated by a major seismic event beneath the sea.

Semi-diurnal tide – One type of astronomical tide that results in two high water and two low water events per day.

Shielding – The term used to describe a shadowing effect during lightning storms when one vessel is blocked from direct lightning strikes by neighboring vessels which are often higher and hence take the direct strike. The shielded vessel may still receive 'secondary' lightning damage via the vessel hit initially.

Shore power – Alternating current, either 115 or 230 volts at 60 Hz frequency, provided by a shore-based power generation source.

Side-tie slip – A linear segment of a marina dock where a vessel may secure its port or starboard side.

Single-slip – Within a marina, a U-shaped configuration that provides a pier on each side of a berthed vessel.

Skiff – A small vessel of wood, fiberglass or metal construction that can be rowed or powered by a motor, typically a small outboard.

Slip – A location for berthing a vessel within a marina. Slips can vary in configuration as discussed herein.

Sloop – A relatively small, single masted sailing vessel.

Sportfishing boat – A well-powered vessel primarily used for game fishing under commercial charter with an experienced Captain and mate. Vessels typically range from 35 to 60 feet, often equipped with a tall tower for spotting surface fish.

Spring line – A line attached from a vessel to a dock, specifically located alongside the vessel to restrict fore and aft movement while the vessel remains in the slip. The spring line also can be an essential line when berthing a vessel as the Captain may use it when turning the vessel.

Spring tide – Periods of two to four days when the range of the astronomical tide is amplified by perfect alignment of the moon and sun, causing intensification of the gravitational pull. Spring tides occur every two weeks but are particularly strong a few times each year.

Squall line – An intense, small-scale meteorological front typically accompanied by high winds and rapid change in atmospheric pressure.

Stray current – In a marina environment, dangerous electrical current inadvertently discharged into the water by a vessel, shore power cord or submerged electrical motor. AC (alternating current) power released as stray current is the primary cause of Electric Shock Drowning.

Sump pump – A type of electrically powered, submersible pump that is used in the bilge of a vessel to discharge waste water overboard. 'Shower sumps' typically collect shower wastewater within a small sealed box that contains a level indicator and pump to discharge the water when the box is filled.

Surge – A sudden and pronounced rise in water level in a coastal environment caused by a variety of natural processes.

Surveyor – A Certified Marine Inspector who conducts visual inspections of vessel components, typically for use by the owner, a potential buyer or an insurance company that provides coverage for the vessel. Surveyors may have specializations such as hull, electrical, engines, etc.

Swim platform – A horizontal platform extending aft from a vessel's transom to provide easy access to the water by swimmers or for launching Personal Water Craft. Some platforms are rigidly fixed to the hull while others are able to lowered and submerged by means of hydraulics powered within the vessel.

T-dock – A marina pier that is shaped as a letter 'T', consisting of a main dock with another pier on the end, positioned perpendicular.

Tenant – In the context of marinas, a tenant is a boat owner who has signed a Marina Tenant Agreement for occupancy of a specific boat slip for berthing of his/her vessel.

Tender – Another name for dinghy and launch, used to transport people and supplies to a larger vessel. Tenders are normally smaller than launches.

Through-hull fitting – A metal or nylon fitting with a hole in the center that is firmly mounted in a vessel's hull to allow liquid wastes to be pumped overboard. An accessible valve inside the hull is attached to the fitting to allow closure when not in use.

Tidal range – The full vertical excursion of water level associated with the tide, measured between levels of high and low water. In contrast, tidal amplitude is measured from the mean water level to either the high- or low-water level and consequently is half the range.

Toys – An informal term representing a variety of Personal Water Craft (PWC) many of which are motorized. Whereas a PWC may represent the only boating unit for some individuals, the term 'Toys' is most commonly used by owners and crew of large yachts who may have a collection of toys (jet skis, kayaks, paddleboards, etc.) aboard for small craft recreation.

Traffic – In the context of this marina guidebook, traffic refers to a congestion of moving vessels typically near the entrance to a major harbor.

Traffic Separation Zone – Near the entrance to major harbors and ports that experience heavy commercial vessel and/or naval traffic, the U.S. Coast Guard has established Traffic Separation Zones and a Separation Scheme to be used by all vessels for preventing collisions and accidents.

Transient slip – A marina slip reserved for vessels that berth for a short stay, typically just a day or two.

Trawler – Two definitions are used within this book: 1) a cabin motor vessel with a high bow and a wheelhouse that is positioned well forward; often used for live-aboard. 2) A commercial fishing vessel that tows large nets at various depths depending upon the intended species targeted.

Tsunami – The general term for large waves that inundate coastal regions at many locations around the globe. They can be generated by a variety of processes, including: subsea earthquakes or seafloor shifts, subsea volcanic eruptions, landslides, glacier calving, meteor impacts, passage of abrupt meteorological storms, etc.

Wharfage – Another (older) term for docking area or berth, most commonly used in association with large vessels for commercial usage.

Yacht Club – A private, non-commercial organization established primarily to promote the sport of racing and cruising. Additionally, Yacht Clubs are a meeting place for nautical folks with similar recreational and social interests. Today, most Yacht Clubs include power boats but some maintain the tradition of sailing vessels only.

Zebra mussel – Similar to Quagga mussels, a species of freshwater mollusk that has been relocated to U.S. waters via ballast water discharged from vessels traveling from western Asian ports. Their rapid colonization has led to major nuisance infestations in the Great Lakes and other U.S. freshwater regions.

Zincs – Molded shapes of solid zinc that are attached to submerged, metal running gear components of vessels to act as sacrificial anodes and minimize galvanic corrosion to key components of the vessel's propulsion system and through-hull fittings.

Author Biography

Scott E. McDowell

Ph.D. – Ocean Physics
Licensed Vessel Captain – U.S. Coast Guard

Dr. McDowell grew up by the sea on Cape Cod in Massachusetts. From an early age he fished for enjoyment then employment through his college years, winning Tuna Tournaments with fish weighing over 600 pounds. After obtaining his Ph.D. in Ocean Physics, he conducted research in the deep North Atlantic Ocean and made the first-ever discovery of 60-mile-wide ocean eddies (thereafter named 'Meddies') swirling a mile below the surface as they moved westward from the Straits of Gibraltar. His discovery spawned international research on mid-ocean eddies for the next two decades.

During his oceanographic career, he led research programs for analysis of currents, tides, waves and water quality characteristics in coastal and deep-ocean environments. Projects ranged from an investigation of seafloor volcanoes at 63 South latitude in the Antarctic Ocean (in 30-ft seas) to studies at the remote Yukon River Delta in the Alaskan Bering Sea and measurements of deep currents affecting submerged gas production platforms in the Gulf of Thailand. He also conducted oceanographic programs for State and U.S. federal agencies, as well as commercial clients worldwide.

Today he enjoys living aboard his 60-ft motor yacht, *Someday Is Now*, in the Florida Keys as a Coast Guard licensed Captain. He's active with a new career of writing non-fiction from his diverse marine experiences, as well as fiction thrillers about nautical espionage and oceanography.

Index

Image courtesy of Horizon Yacht